OCEAN LINERS

The Golden Years

"The Arrival" (1914) by the English painter C.R.W. Nevinson. His exhibition of war pictures in 1916 was the first of its kind and led to the appointment of other war artists. Nevinson, once described as a "high class journalist in paint", here captures his subject to perfection.

OCEAN LINERS

The Golden Years

A PICTORIAL ANTHOLOGY
COMPILED BY
RUPERT PRIOR

TIGER BOOKS INTERNATIONAL
LONDON

TO THE MEMORY OF DENNIS LENNON CBE MC

First published in Great Britain 1993 by
Tiger Books International PLC
London

ISBN 1-85501-343-6

British Library Cataloguing in Publication Data is available
from the British Library.

This book was conceived, edited, designed and produced by
Morgan Samuel Editions,
11 Uxbridge Street, London W8 7TQ

Typesetting by Pre-Press Ltd, London.
Printed and bound by Poligrafici
Calderara S.p.a, Bologna, Italy.

CONTENTS

PROLOGUE

THE DECORATION OF OCEAN LINERS

Arthur J. Davis, 1922
R.I.B.A. Journal

This subject covers such a large field, and its ramifications are so numerous, that I fear that in the short time at my disposal it would be impossible to deal adequately with all its details. I propose, therefore, to confine myself to broad principles, and pass on to the beginning of the nineteenth century, when steam was first introduced in navigation, and the *Charlotte Dundas*, constructed by Symington, was launched on the Forth and Clyde canal.

She carried an engine, designed by the great James Watt, that drove a stern wheel. Her success inspired the American engineer, Robert Fulton, to build the *Clermont*, in New York, five years later. This vessel, also engined by Watt, travelled up the Hudson River from New York to Albany, performing the journey of 130 miles in thirty-two hours. We are told that an enormous and, on the whole, sceptical crowd gathered to witness the commencement of what was to prove a classic voyage. According to an account written in the New York *Evening Sun*, the *Clermont* "moved out into the stream, the steam connection hissing at the joints, the crude machinery thumping and groaning, the wheels splashing and the smoke-stack belching like a volcano," while "one honest countryman, after beholding the unaccountable object from the shore, ran home and told his wife that he had seen the devil on his way to Albany in a saw mill".

That was in the year 1807, but it was not until 24 May 1819, when the *Savannah*, a wooden sailing ship fitted with an auxiliary steam engine, quitted the port which bears her name, and a fortnight later steamed slowly up the Mersey, to the astonishment of a large crowd of spectators, that the Atlantic steamer service may be said to have received its effective initial impulse. Nothing, perhaps, has contributed more largely than this to the maintenance of cordial relations between Anglo-Saxons in the old and new worlds, and to the extraordinary developments which have since been effected in transatlantic travel. Our great-grandfathers seemed to have scarcely realised the consummate importance of the new departure.

The *Britannia*, the pioneer vessel of the Cunard fleet, measured 207 feet long by 34 feet broad and 22 feet deep, with a tonnage burden of 1,154 and an indicated horse-power of 740. Her cargo capacity was 225 tons, and she was fitted to accommodate 115 cabin passengers, but had no steerage. Her average speed was 8–knots per hour on a coal consumption of 38 tons per day. In her passenger list, eighteen months after her maiden voyage, we find the name of Charles Dickens, and in an account of his crossing he writes:

"I had been led by certain highly-coloured illustrations to anticipate a saloon, 'furnished in a style of more than Eastern splendour, filled (but not inconveniently so) with groups of ladies and gentlemen in the very highest state of enjoyment and vivacity', but I was terribly disappointed with the reality, which I can only compare to a gigantic hearse with windows in the side".

One can easily imagine what would have been the surprise of "Boz" at the appearance of a modern ship, with its wireless telegraphy, electric light, gymnasia, swimming bath, and even a journal such as the *Cunard Bulletin* printed and published during the voyage.

This development has taken the form of a geometric progression, but it is only within the last twenty years that one can say that the ocean liner, with all her wonderful display of technical and artistic equipment, has reached her present state of perfection.

It is difficult to appreciate the full debt which the science and art of shipbuilding owe to the individual enterprise of such men as

Samuel Cunard, William Inman, Thomas Ismay and Alexander Allan.

It was Thomas Ismay who realised, in the year 1875, that the old tradition of placing passengers aft made for acute discomfort with the arrival of the screw propeller, and he decided to put his passenger quarters forward of the engine rooms, where the vibration and movement of the vessel were least noticeable. The saloons and staterooms were placed amidships, and the former were constructed to occupy the whole width of the vessel, being superior in ventilation and lighting to any yet in existence.

It was in the spring of 1913 that the *Aquitania*, at once the latest and the greatest of marine wonders, glided from her berth into the same waters which, little more than a century ago, witnessed the first feeble efforts of Bell's *Comet*. To-day, it is almost impossible to picture this tiny vessel of 1812 by the side of the colossus of 1914, with accommodation for 3,250 passengers, together with a crew of 1,000; a floating population larger than that of many English towns.

Of the White Star liner *Olympic* it has been said that she is not so much a ship as a palatial floating hotel, with every luxury that modern decoration and furnishing can provide; indeed, the simile of the floating hotel is somewhat inadequate; the term "Floating Town" more precisely describes her construction.

Think of all the historic ships which you have ever heard of, from the time of Columbus's *Santa Maria*, Grenville's *Revenge*, Nelson's *Victory*, even through that interesting maritime period of the old East Indiamen and the clipper-ship. Consider, if you will, the whole category of epoch-making steamships, from the time that Papin discovered steam power; consider Fulton's *Clermont*, the Clyde-built *Comet*, the famous *Great Eastern*, down to the *Mauretania* and the *Majestic*, and then you can readily realise the continuous advance that has been made in the construction and equipment of that modern marvel "the transatlantic liner".

These colossal vessels have caused shipyards and piers to undergo considerable enlargement, and have required harbours to be deeply dredged.

An inspection of the interior of the *Olympic*, means a walk of no less than nine miles. It is more than a third of a mile round her deck, and

Elevation and detail for the interior decoration of the *Otranto,* delivered in 1926, by Andrew Noble Prentice for the Orient Line. Designs are for a wall decoration incorporating lacquer panels (probably for the card room).

from waterline to bridge she is about as high as a six-storey building. She has eleven steel decks, seven of which are used by passengers. The two sets of reciprocating engines, each driving a wing shaft, whilst the middle screw is driven by a turbine, are the largest ever built.

Each of the funnels is wide enough to take two railway trains running abreast, and they rise 81 feet above the deck.

This rapid development has brought about a complete revolution in the methods employed both as regards the internal planning and the equipment of these ships. With the inevitable necessity of specialising in many new directions, it has become the practice to employ experts to advise upon the various requirements of the modern liner, and not only does this apply to the actual planning of the habitable portion of the ship, but also to her decoration, furniture, electric light, heating, ventilation and lift installations. As the natural sequence of this evolution, so far as the purely non-nautical construction is concerned, it was found that the ship designers could no longer deal adequately with the large areas and surfaces to be planned. The space for the important public rooms was so vast, and the height of the rooms so great, that the expert knowledge of the architect was necessary to deal effectively with the arrangements of these available spaces.

As an experiment the architect was first introduced chiefly as an art adviser, and it was considered that his duties should be confined within the limits of decoration and furniture. Having justified his appointment, he gradually encroached on other portions of the ship, and it has now been found advisable to bring him into contact with the ship-architect at the very early stages of the design. As I have heard it put rather appropriately, the ship is now in the hands of the wet and the dry architects. All the parts of her construction affecting her main lines, the great sweep of her bows, the laying of her keel, her superstructure and her navigating qualities, are naturally in the hands of the "wet" architect, whereas the "dry" architect is called in and consulted when it comes to planning her inside and finishing her

public rooms and cabins. The method pursued by the great shipping companies is roughly as follows.

After they have decided upon the size, tonnage, and carrying capacity of the ship they intend to build, they invite tenders from the various shipbuilding yards. The contract having been agreed upon, and the builders having been appointed, the architect is next consulted. At this stage the position of the bulkheads, funnel casting, expansion joints, cargo hatches, etc., are virtually settled; but the spaces remaining still available for the planning of the principal public rooms, staircases, elvators, staterooms, and service offices have to be dealt with. Here is where the architect begins his work. It must, however, be clearly understood that he is only called in to work out the interior scheme of the vessel in collaboration with the ship-designer, to whose knowledge of the laws governing marine construction he must necessarily defer.

All the features with which we have long been familiar in our great hotels and public buildings are at the disposal of the architect in the planning and decorative equipment of the modern liner. So numerous are the rooms, so

8

great the area, and so increased in available height that it has now not only become possible but necessary to employ the recognised rules of architectural planning.

The displacement of our modern ships has recently been increased approximately from 15,000 to 50,000 tons. These figures are in themselves a proof that many arrangements which were useful and even necessary in the past to cope with the requirements of a vessel half-submerged, are altogether out of place on a mighty liner of a length of over 900 feet, a width of 97 feet, and with its upper decks towering some 60 feet above the water level.

In the public rooms of small vessels, light and air are obtainable solely through the circular ports, which can only be manipulated by persons in authority, and which in stormy weather are hermetically sealed. As a consequence, that peculiar atmosphere is created in which the odours of oil, stale cooking, and general stuffiness all combine with the incessant vibration to impress persons of delicate susceptibility that the pleasures of ocean travel are by no means always equal to the stationary comforts of dry land. In the past conditions such as these have deterred many

from undertaking long journeys by sea. All this has been entirely altered on the great liner. The port-holes have vanished from the upper decks, and have been replaced by large sash and casement windows, operated with ease by either passenger or steward. Nor is this all; when these windows are shut, the natural air is replaced by an efficient and complete scheme of artificial ventilation, a supply of air at any desired temperature being forced to every part of the ship.

Again, the immense addition to the tonnage of modern ships, although it has involved an increase in the size of the engines, coal bunkers, cargo and funnel hatches, etc., has not done so in a ratio proportionate to the addition of extra space available for the public rooms, the extent of which has been thus greatly increased. For instance, it is now possible to obtain long vistas through complete suites planned in the grand manner, even monumental and picturesque architectural effects being thus rendered possible.

It may not be uninteresting to give a short list of the public rooms required for the first-class accommodation of an Atlantic liner such as the *Berengaria*, *Majestic*, or the *Aquitania*, each of which has eight floors or decks, communicating with one another by elevators, as well as several staircases. On the lower decks, in addition to the many staterooms, cabins, kitchens, and service rooms, etc., we find the great dining saloon (capable of seating from 500 to 600 persons), with an adjoining grill-room, foyer, and lounge, a large swimming bath and gymnasium, Turkish and electric baths, and purser's office, etc. Above, on the upper decks, in addition to the main staircase and several lifts, we find the ladies' drawing room and writing room, a hall, lounge, and ballroom, the veranda cafe, smoking room, exhibition gallery, barber's shop, book and flowerstalls, while on the converted German liners a restaurant and winter garden were features of considerable prominence.

It has been recognised that every class of passenger expects to be provided with all the latest improvements, and while before the war competition among the various shipping

9

companies was so keen, it was obvious that neither expense nor trouble could be spared to provide every comfort to all classes on board. Not only are new suggestions constantly elaborated, but everybody interested in the success of a new ship is encouraged to bring forward any fresh solution to the many problems, which vary with every vessel launched.

The once familiar "cabin" has no longer a place in the vocabulary of the great shipping companies. The term stateroom has a dignified sound more appropriate to these luxurious rooms. Frequently arranged in suites containing a sitting room, bedroom, and bathroom, with the addition sometimes of a private dining room, these apartments are the last word in comfort and refinement. In the bedrooms, double or single beds, made of some rare wood, oxidized silver, or brass, replace the old awkward bunks placed one above the other. Finely veneered woods, panelled and delicately tinted walls, light washable materials for curtains and furniture coverings, and decorations free from all unnecessary elaboration, are as much the special feature of these rooms as the wardrobes, fittings and cupboards, which are replete with every possible convenience.

The artificially ventilated inside cabin, so often and so rightly objected to, is gradually disappearing, and ingenious arrangements are now contrived to enable even the innermost staterooms to receive fresh air and light, thus considerably enhancing their letting value.

All the fittings of these cabins are especially thought out and constructed for practical utility, the style of decoration selected for the room being maintained throughout.

Methods of design, appropriate when used in connection with buildings, cannot be transposed without change and adaptation to the requirements of sea-going vessels.

The pitfalls to be avoided are legion, and many schemes which look very well on paper may prove to be failures when put into execution. Decorations, for instance, should not be designed without full consideration being given to the sheer and camber, which in

Perspective of the *Orion,* built for the Australian service. For the first time in the history of shipbuilding an architect, Brian O'Rorke, was called upon to carry out the entire decoration of the ship. A complete air-conditioning plant was installed on the *Orion,* the first liner to be thus equipped, and Bakelite and chromium were used extensively as they are unaffected by sea air.

certain portions of a ship are considerable. It is occasionally noticeable that inexperienced decorators arrange the cornices of a large room to follow the "camber" of the underside of the deck line above, while overdoors, window bars, and dado mouldings are arranged horizontally. The effect thus produced is extremely unpleasant, and far more noticeable in execution than on the drawings.

Another temptation to be avoided is to overcrowd a room with heavy ornament and meretricious decoration. This fault was very apparent on some of the earlier German liners, where refinement of detail was often sacrificed to tawdry magnificence and over-elaboration.

On a ship, people are imprisoned together for days, and sometimes weeks; forced to live a life altogether different from that to which they are accustomed on land. They are frequently compelled to look to the ship herself to provide them with interest and entertainment during an often tedious voyage. It is the duty of the architect to provide suitable surroundings, combining an air of comfort and repose in the appearance of the different rooms, which, it may be added, are often of necessity seen under unpleasant conditions.

Again, the factor of relative scale is of paramount importance. It is a well-recognised axiom that no matter how large the rooms to be dealt with on a ship may be, somehow the scale appears much smaller than that of a room of similar dimensions on land. The probable explanation of this is that the absence of heavy constructional piers, deep window and door recesses, etc., tends to diminish the monumental character. Hence heavy or incongruous ornament looks doubly out of place when applied to the comparatively light construction of a ship.

Although the average life of a great liner may be assumed to be only about fifteen years, all the material and workmanship used in the construction must be of the very finest quality. Of late a great number of experiments have been made with new materials. Many of these have stood with remarkable success the severe tests to which they have been subjected, and there seems to be no limit to future possibilities in this direction. There has been some prejudice, especially among foreign companies, against the employment of plaster ceilings, but in ships such as the *Mauretania*, *Laconia*, *Alsatia* and *Olympic*, where such ceilings have been tested, they have been entirely satisfactory.

Other decorative materials – such as stucco, tiles, mosaic, *scagliola* and trellis – may also be used with discretion; but marble and brickwork should be avoided on account of their weight, not only in appearance, but in fact. The marine designer is obliged to give special consideration to this question, particularly on the upper decks. It is unfair, therefore, to handicap him with heavy or bulky materials, which may easily necessitate revision of calculations and involve an increase in the strength of the supporting structure.

Vibration at sea is also an extremely serious question in fast-going vessels, and materials which are likely to scale off or crack should be avoided. A ship is designed primarily to be in motion, and, further, a vessel not merely moves forward, but is subject to lateral roll and a countless number of other strains. This applies not only to the vessel herself and every object she carries, but also to her human freight. The two principal movements are pitching and rolling, and, although the latter has been minimised on vessels of recent construction where such innovations as anti-rolling tanks have been installed, these movements are still felt to a considerable extent in bad weather. As the horizontal section through the centre of the hull of a ship much resembles the shape of an elongated cigar, the pitch or plunging movement is naturally less noticeable than the lateral roll. It is wise, therefore, to design all the swimming tanks and baths so that their length is parallel to the long axis of the vessel, the movement of the water they contain trying to regain its own level being thus minimised. The same remark applies equally to the planning of staircases and companion-ways, which are easier to negotiate in bad weather when the direction is fore and aft, or, in other words, parallel to that in which the ship is moving. In these staircases, which should be

substantially balustraded, and not too wide, it is advisable to avoid winders, as well as awkward turns. Easy flights with comfortable landings are virtually essential.

Conditions at sea are often very unpleasant, and passengers, after braving the elements on the exposed decks, or sitting for hours on the promenade gazing at a far remote horizon, are only too glad to return to a cheerful room with comfortable surroundings and, for a time at least, forget they are at sea. This remark will explain the desirability of introducing suitable fireplaces wherever possible, even though they only supplement the heating installation.

The standard material used for painted woodwork on board a modern liner is well-seasoned Honduras mahogany; but Cuban mahogany, teak, oak, satinwood, walnut, black bean, and many other varieties of hardwoods are often used for decorative purposes.

The floors, which are for the most part covered with a thick cork carpet over a layer of magnesite composition, are not infrequently laid with wood parquetry fixed to creosoted fillets. The principal rooms and cabins are partially covered with fine rugs and carpets, and the vestibules, gangways, and stairs by a non-slip rubber tiling or cork carpet.

It is of course impossible to lay down any golden rule as to what style or styles are the most suitable for a liner. Of recent years several attempts have been made to decorate all the rooms in the vogue of one particular period; but, although by no means unsuccessful, such treatment tends rather to monotony, and a variety is, therefore, more generally preferable.

Perhaps the best examples of Jacobean, Restoration, Georgian, Regency, Louis XV, Louis XVI, Adam, and Empire, if simply treated, are amongst the most suitable.

In the old liners the motion at sea was so considerable that every article of furniture had to be permanently screwed to the floors. The chairs were nearly always of the heavy inconvenient pattern revolving on a central axis, and, in a crowded dining saloon, had to be placed so near to each other that a gymnastic feat was often necessary in order to negotiate a seat at the table. During meals

"fiddles" were a frequent necessity, all plates, decanters and glasses having special compartments to prevent their skidding or upsetting. To-day, however, the arrangement of the furniture is in all respects similar to that usual in a modern hotel. While every variety of table, settee, chair and sofa is to be found in the principal rooms, with the exception of the larger fittings every article of furniture is movable, and only screwed down when the weather is exceptionally rough.

In the dining saloons the long *table d'hôte* table has been eliminated, and gives way to a series of small convertible tables, which are readily extended and enlarged, so that passengers can arrange their own parties. All the china and glass are now as dainty as that of the private home, and the greatest care is taken in the choice of suitable replicas of old Worcester, Crown Derby, Wedgwood and Sèvres, so as to harmonise with specially designed reproductions or adaptions of antique silver and old plate of the period chosen.

It is not to the details of the catering departments alone that the care of the expert and the connoisseur is confined. In all the public rooms will be found choice replicas and even originals of the Old Masters, as well as mezzotints, prints, and reproductions of notable excellence. The catalogue of works of art and interest to be found on board one of the latest vessels would be at least equal to that of many a small art gallery.

It may not be out of place to give a short description of the work and the useful services that these great ships rendered in the war. As fighting ships, hospital ships and transports they fully justified all the expectations that were predicted of them (e.g. the wonderful work that was done in transporting the entire American army across the broad Atlantic). A Cunarder, designed and equipped for the peaceful transport of passengers and goods was converted into an efficient war weapon and fought a successful duel with the *Cap Trafalgar*, a ship of similar type.

To the *Carmania* fell this singular honour, and five years' war at sea produced few more kindling and romantic stories.

This is but one illustration among many of what these ships could do when stripped of their peace clothing and equipped in the stern accoutrements of war. Such exploits as that of the *Carmania* and the never-to-be forgotten sinking of the *Lusitania*, which was principally instrumental in bringing the United States into the war, cannot be ignored when dealing with the history of the ocean liner. The sacrifices that the British shipping companies made were enormous, and can only be realised when one is informed that the losses in tonnage of a company such as the Cunard Line during the war were approximately 65 per cent of their entire fleet; the other important companies suffering to a similar extent.

Long before the conclusion of hostilities the German submarine menace was well in hand, and new ships were being put on the stocks to replace the ill fated vessels that had been sunk by the enemy. These post-war ships, some of which are now launched and ploughing the high seas, are designed on a somewhat different plan. The principal innovation is one which has fundamentally altered its main lines: I am referring to the use of oil instead of coal as a fuel. The introduction of this new method has greatly decreased the time expended in replenishing the fuel supplies, as a ship can now be refitted for her return journey in a few hours, whereas in the older vessels the coaling process takes several days; moreover, all the dirt and dust caused by the coaling is eliminated and the decorations and fittings are kept in better condition.

Owing to the new immigration laws which have been passed in the United States, the fourth class, or steerage, accommodation is no longer of the same importance as in more prosperous days. Fares have increased in proportion to the cost of construction, and many innovations have been introduced to cope with the altered requirements of the present-day trade. Naturally, these requirements change each year.

In ship construction the British designer holds the first place in the world's estimation. The vessels which have been built on the Clyde, the Tyne or the Lagan , whether they be battleship, liner or tramp, bear the stamp which marks them as being the aristocrats of the sea.

The reputation of our naval *confréres* is so high that it is for us architects who are entrusted with the decorations of the interior of their ships to see that this standard is maintained throughout,and that our joint labours are worthy of that genius for naval construction which commands the admiration of the world.

I can remember the days of travel to the East, more than forty years ago, in the old P. and O. liners, very fine seaworthy vessels but very uncomfortable to live in. Dark, evil-smelling, ill-ventilated, the cabins opened into the saloon where meals were taken, so that everything that went on in the saloon was heard in the cabins, and *vice versa*. That is a trying experience which no longer occurs to one making a voyage to the Far East or elsewhere in one of these great vessels.

May I point out that when I was first engaged, some 15 years ago, to start this work, I said to the directors of the company who employed me: "Why don't you make a ship look like a ship?". The answer I was given was that the people who use these ships are not pirates; they do not dance hornpipes; they are mostly seasick American ladies, and the one thing they want to forget when they are on the vessel is that they are on a ship at all. The people who travel on these large ships are the people who live in hotels; they are not ships for sailors or for yachtsmen or for people who enjoy the sea. They are inhabited by all sorts of people, some of whom are very delicate and stay in their cabin during the whole voyage; others, less delicate, stay in the smoke-room all through the voyage. The programme of trans-Atlantic travel as it exists to-day is a very peculiar one. I suggest to you that the trans-Atlantic liner is not merely a ship, she is a floating town with 3,000 passengers of all kinds, with all sorts of tastes, and those who enjoy being there are distinctly in the minority. If we could get ships to look inside like ships, and get people to enjoy the sea, it would be a very good thing; but all we can do, as things are, is to give them gigantic floating hotels.

14

The proposed first class lounge for the motor liner *Manoora*. Early passenger carrying vessels were poorly furnished and had little or no decoration. British shipowners were slow in applying art to the passenger vessel but once they realised its scope and power, ship-furnishing developed with amazing rapidity and the ocean liner was admired as much for the luxury of its appointments as for its speed. The architect responsible for this perspective is A.N. Prentice.

The historic Compagnie Générale Transatlantique, founded in France in 1864, likened its vessels to the best hotels in France. The company began operations following the award of a mail-carriage contract to New York and the Caribbean.

SOVEREIGNS OF THE SEA

"the motion of the ship precludes
carrying the older red wines"

First Class menu of the *Aquitania*

Gallery of the Orient liner *Orion*. Her designers regarded her as an ocean liner, not a "floating hotel". Alcoves contained writing desks while armchairs and sofas, with occasional tables, allowed passengers to sit without disturbance from passing feet. The rugs are by Marion Dorn.

Inset: Study of an entrance hall from the archives of the Union-Castle Mail Steamship Company. Furniture on early passenger ships was of the horse-hair bench variety, but within fifty years ocean liners outstripped hotels in comfort and luxury.

THE ARCHITECTURE OF THE SHIP
Architect's Journal 1922

Steel and steam have revolutionised the building of ships, and "the great wall-sided liner" has a beauty all its own, while it is in the interior that the greatest changes have occurred. The smoky cabins with their swinging lamps, in which one could never forget, even in dead calm, that one was at sea, have been succeeded by the Corinthian-columned, white-marbled, soft-carpeted and rubber-floored saloons of the ocean greyhounds of to-day. The savour of the sea does not penetrate; the ship's bell is not heard. Wherefore most passengers sail unmindful of the perils of the deep that encompass them, and only the sudden stopping of the engines can give them any alarm.

By the use of familiar and traditional forms such as column, architrave and entablature, a feeling of land security is created which gives the unwilling seafarer the atmosphere, if not of his home, then of his hotel. Perhaps in a few years our great ships will float as smoothly as though on rails.

We have had the "gin-palace" design, and we have had the "period" design; shall we not, by intimate realization of what a ship is, in the future be able to arrive at the "ship" design? Modern construction is, unfortunately, upsetting all the accepted art forms. And a modern liner being what it is, a thing of steel plates and girders and rivets, it would seem to be no worse to clothe it with plaster and paint in one of the orthodox land styles, than to affect some sentimental sea style reminiscent of Trafalgar and the "wooden walls".

It is quite clear, however, that a very good opening for original treatment presents itself. Stringers and iron-frames, garboard strake and web-frame, foremast and wire-stays, iron keels and deck-beams, side-plates and rivets – is there no inspiration in these out of which something new might be born? And the bow? Ruskin tells us that the sum of navigation is in that. "That rude simplicity of bent plank, that can breast its way through the death that is in the deep sea, has in it the soul of shipping.

Beyond this, we may have more work, more men, more money; we cannot have more miracles ... The boat's bow is naïvely perfect; complete without an effort ... You may magnify it or decorate it as you will; you will not add to the wonder of it. Lengthen it into hatchet-like edge of iron, strengthen it with complex tracery of ribs of oak, carve it and gild it till a column of light moves beneath it on the sea, you have made no more of it than it was at first."

BUILDING A LINER
A. C. Hardy

When the architect of a vessel has finished his preliminary work the construction begins, entailing skill and labour that may endure from six months to six years.

The first stage in the construction of a ship begins with the laying of the keel in the shipyard, a function which may or may not be accompanied by ceremony, according to the nature of the ship and her subsequent duties. It continues until the time of the launch.

The launch marks the end of stage one and the beginning of stage two – the vessel's partial entry into the world, her emergence, as it were, from the embryo stage. Part two is concerned with the fitting-out, which is generally done in the basin alongside a large crane that lifts on board all kinds of items from heavy machinery down to small ventilating fans.

With the exception of the launch, stage three is the most important and anxious of all from the point of view of the naval architect. It is the trial trip, for then the ship must prove herself; she must make the speed which the design conditions have laid down; she must make it, furthermore, at a certain draught and with a certain specified fuel consumption in pounds per horsepower developed per hour, or in tons of fuel used per twenty-four hours. At this stage, too, she must demonstrate her ability to steer properly, to pull up from "full speed ahead" to "stop", and to go from "full speed ahead" to "full speed astern" in a prescribed time. The launch is an anxious moment because, if calculations have gone wrong, the vessel may turn over or,

alternatively, she may damage herself in running down the ways. Even so, she is not a completed ship and repairs may in certain circumstances be effected. On the trial trip, however, the vessel must be accepted or rejected by the owners. Thanks to the accuracy of modern ship construction the percentage of rejections per thousand ships built is almost negligible.

The fourth stage is concerned with the active life of the ship. So great is the progress of modern machinery and the ability of the marine engineer to give more and more speed without corresponding increase in fuel consumption, that the life of a ship is tending to shorten, not because the hull is worn out, but because it is economically obsolete.

The final stage of which we can speak is the "death" of the ship. She then passes into the ship-breaker's hands and suffers the reverse process. Ironically enough, in many instances the same tools are employed in the breaking; but, whereas building is a matter for precision

Entrance to the Music saloon of the P. & O. *Maloga* (1911). Ship-furnishing was based primarily on one of the oldest arts of all, the furnishing of the home. At the turn of the century passenger vessels were equipped in much the same way as a typical well-to-do house.

19

The *Great Eastern,* in her day one of the world's largest ships. Designed by Isambard Brunel, the famous engineer, and John Scott Russell, the *Great Eastern* was laid down in May 1853. A series of misfortunes befell her, everyone associated with her lost money, and she subsequently found work as a cable ship. A notable experiment, her huge hull looms large in the story of the steamship.

and care in adjustment of parts, the breaking of ships is aimed rather at getting the largest pieces of metal consistent with the requirements of the furnaces into which these parts will ultimately be fed. Thus, the "dust to dust" of the human body is repeated all over again in the "iron to iron" of the death of a ship.

In what some people are pleased to call the halcyon days of ship-building – before 1914 – it was possible for a piece of iron ore to come in at the quays on the Tyne, be transformed into pig-iron in the blast furnaces and thence to be transferred to the big steel smelting furnaces. It would subsequently be transformed into an angle-bar or a plate, taken to the shipyard, measured, punched, sheared, hung up on the ship's structure, riveted, caulked, painted and sent away to sea as a small part of the complete vessel.

Changing economic conditions have now ruled out all that. There are many shipbuilding companies in some way or another financially associated with steel companies. For this reason they buy the products of those steel companies.

Importance of Building Berths

Ships cannot be erected at random anywhere near water. They are built on ground which is specially prepared and which often has been used for the purpose for as many as upwards of one hundred years. The building berth is in some ways the most vital factor in the construction of a ship, for it has to take a continually increasing weight of hull structure.

More important still, it has to take the weight of the structure and support the hull members, the floors, frames and the like, when they are in a relatively "plastic" state one to the other. The ground must therefore be solid, not liable to subside under weathering, or when heavy weights such as large castings are put into position on the structure. Any shifting of the ground not only means endless work in putting members back in their relative positions, but it may also entail serious distortion to the hull of the ship. For this reason, naval architects are always anxious when there is any postponement in the construction of a vessel that has been begun, particularly if the vessel's hull is not completely plated, i.e. made rigid.

Building blocks made of baulks of timber, pitch-pine or fir, are placed alternately in thwartship and fore-and-aft positions, being first of all arranged on pitch-pine planks running longitudinally down the building berth. Two blocks are then placed athwartships at a distance apart from centre to centre, varying with the size of the ship, then two more are arranged on top of these and at right angles to them. This is generally repeated with another "collection" of fore-and-aft and thwartship blocks: and then on top of these is a further layer of wood, and, finally, a tapered cap piece, shaped for insertion of wedges under the keel plates for purposes of "setting up" or lowering the plates themselves. Many of the modern shipyards with completely concrete berths use concrete blocks, but the principles employed are the same.

Ships are always built on a declivity to the berth. But it is necessary first to arrange that the tops of all the building blocks from the forward end of the vessel to the aft end shall be at this declivity, i.e. that the line of the top of the caps shall slope to the horizontal, at a rate of nine-sixteenths of an inch to the foot. When the blocks have been "levelled", as it is called, in this way, the first of the flat plate keel units is taken and put down on the blocks, this having been prepared previously in the platers' shed.

The keel plates, as with all other plates used in ship construction, have been ordered from

The M class *Morea* in a graving (or dry) dock. A watercolour by B.F. Gribble, maritime historian and marine painter to the Worshipful Company of Shipwrights. Built in Glasgow for P. & O., the *Morea* entered service in 1908 and was used on Australian and Far Eastern routes. The ocean giants could be dry docked so quickly that an overhaul involved only a temporary stop in their schedule.

the rolling mills by the shipyard drawing office to a rough size and shape, slightly larger than the size required. The plater has taken the plate from a "rack", as it is called – where all plates are stacked vertically – and, working to the plan of the flat plate keel which he has received from the drawing office, has marked it for shearing, punching, planing and any other physical operations that may be necessary.

The complete set of keel plates is taken one by one to the building berth and each plate is lifted on to the blocks by the overhead cranes, being lowered into its proper place according to the sequence numbers. Each plate is joined to its neighbour by means of a butt strap – that is to say, the two ends of the plate are placed touching each other. Over them is placed another plate of the same width as the keel plate, but only long enough to cover the single, double or triple row of rivet holes at the end of each keel plate. This is known as a butt strap in contradistinction to a butt lap, by which latter term is meant that one end of the plate is lapped over another, the holes in the ends being common and riveted through.

The keel plates are all "centred" on the blocks by the shipwrights, who make sure that the steel is straight end for end, and that it is tolerably level. Although the keel plates are now in position and bolted together, the whole keel is by no means rigid, but, as soon as it has been laid and levelled, it is riveted. The fore and aft angle bars for the vertical keel are then bolted into position. An angle bar is, as the name indicates, a long length of steel sectioned as a right angle.

After these angle bars have been placed in position a start is made with the placing in position of the vertical keel. This, with the flat plate keel forms the backbone of the ship. It has other angle bars attached at the top, and vertical ones on either side. It is to these vertical angle bars that the floors, as they are called, are next attached. These are the vertical thwartship members which at the ship's centre are the same depth as the height of the vertical keel. When plating has been placed underneath them, on top and along the sides, they form the ship's double bottom, a

receptacle for water ballast, for liquid fuel, and for lubricating oil. It also acts as a powerful protection against damage, should the ship ground; for it means that even if the outer bottom is pierced, the vessel can still float on the inner bottom or tank tops. The floors are generally lightened by means of manholes which are punched into them. In addition to lightening the plate, the manhole also has the effect of making the tank capable of carrying liquid. Where it is desired to complete a tank, then the floors are solid.

Our "members" now comprise a flat plate keel, vertical keel and floors. These floors have to be kept at the right distance, the one from the other, by means of other plates which are called intercostals (i.e. "between the ribs"). They are so called because they extend only from one floor to the next. They contribute to the longitudinal strength of the ship and are placed in position after all the floors have been arranged. By this time, too, a start has been made with the outer bottom plating, and the tank top itself is nearly complete, as well as the plating at the tank side.

We now have the main fore and aft skeleton or backbone of the ship. It remains only to add what the old shipwrights knew as the ribs, i.e. the frames. These are made of one or another of various sections – bulb bar, angle bar, or even "Z" bar, the names being according to the sections, and the sections used according to the type of ship. These frames are attached to the tank side – which has small angle-bar brackets at intervals corresponding to the frame spacing of the ship – by means of large brackets that are generally known as knees.

The frames themselves, according to the type of ship, are either straight up and down or curved. In any event, they generally curve at the bilge of the ship, i.e. the rounded portion between the outer bottom and the ship's side.

By this time a start has been made with placing the shell plating in position. Several of the deck plates have also been "laid"; but the plating of the deck is not yet complete, for many apertures will have been left, the biggest one being for the machinery. There are also other apertures corresponding to the cargo

22

holds. The number of tiers of beams will depend upon the number of decks in the ship, eight or nine in the largest ships. If the vessel is a large passenger liner, a start will now have been made on the superstructure.

Ready for the Launch

While all this constructional work has been going on, the big castings for the stem and stern frame will have been lifted in position and will now be incorporated in the hull itself. If the ship is a twin-screw vessel with a rounded stern – known as a cruiser stern – then the stern frame castings may be large and in certain instances rather complicated. The apertures for the twin screws are sometimes known, because of their appearance, as "spectacle frames".

The different categories of workmen are continually following one another throughout the ship. The carpenters have been first, with the platers, to lay the keel and see that the preliminary members of the ship are in place. More platers have followed the carpenters, the riveters are following the platers, and the caulkers are following the riveters. The task of the riveters is to see that the plates are water tight. The caulkers are followed by gangs of testers, to test the tanks for water-tightness – to Lloyd's or other Classification Society requirements – against so many feet head of water. This having been done, the compartments inside and out can be dried and will be ready for painting. By this time, too, the carpenters will be back on the job again, laying the launch-way beneath the hull.

The launching of a ship is a highly specialized performance; suffice it to say, by now, however, that the vessel will be sufficiently riveted, caulked and made watertight for consideration to be given to her entry into the water. She slides down the way into the water, floats at a very light draught successfully, is taken in hand by tugs, and towed alongside the fitting-out basin to receive, first of all, her machinery.

In many ships a start may already have been made on this when the ship is on the stocks. Even should the boilers be in place, however, there will still be a great deal of out-fitting to be done in the way of accommodation, cargo gear, masts, funnels, derricks, and so on. Generally the heavy machinery is lifted on board piece by piece, and is built up much in the same way as the hull itself has been built up, i.e. from the bottom. Until all this is in position and the engine-room is virtually complete it is impossible to finish the upper portion of the hull and to lower the engine-room hatch or top in place.

Once this has been done, the work on the equipment of the ship will have been pressed forward to such an extent that little remains to be done but the putting on board of the equipment. This includes boats, lifebelts and the like, and the finishing off of the joiner work in the cabins. After this the ship will be ready for the first of her many important ventures – the trial trip at sea. The time taken for all this conventional work varies. A small ship may be built in six months. A large vessel may take as long as six years. This is particularly true with mammoth transatlantic liners, for here considerations of policy and even of politics sometimes affect the construction as much as the plates and steel work.

For lounging and tippling: a soda fountain on board the *Aquitania*, 1923. Shipboard drinking was exempt from the excise duty imposed ashore and on a single voyage on the *Queen Mary,* for example, some 5,000 bottles of spirits, 10,000 bottles of wine, 40,000 bottles of beer and 60,000 bottles of mineral water would be consumed.

LAUNCHING CEREMONIES
Frank C. Bowen

The launching and christening ceremony is the great event in a ship's career. No matter how great a name she may make for herself afterwards, or how many records she may break, the memory of all who attended her launching will inevitably return to that first occasion when she slid down the ways, gradually gathering momentum. The moment when she took the water and made her curtsy to the guests at the head of the slip before she surrendered herself to the care of the attendant tugs will be long remembered. However many launching ceremonies may have been experienced, most spectators will still know a thrill as they see a ship go down the ways.

No matter what country it may be, Eastern or Western, the launch of a ship is always the occasion of a picturesque and impressive ceremony. Even among the maritime nations which have adopted identical shipbuilding machinery and scientific procedure for bringing the ship to the launching stage, the specific details of the ceremony vary according to the spirit and temperament of the people.

In most countries, however, the ceremony is only a variation of that familiar in Great Britain. The personage asked to sponsor the ship stands on a platform built round her bow as she rests on the slipway. At the exact moment that the tide serves to let the ship take the water, the sponsor breaks a bottle of wine over the vessel's stem, wishes good luck to her and to those who sail in her, operates the machinery that releases her and lets her slide down the ways.

There is room in this ceremony for many modifications. Sometimes the bottle of wine is suspended from the bow of the ship by a white silken ribbon, so that the sponsor has only to let go for it to fall against the ship's side. Sometimes it is held in the hand to break, a method that is apt to scatter wine over the launching party; and sometimes the bottle rests in a cradle against the bow of the ship, held down against a strong spring. The moment a

button is pressed, the spring is released and the bottle is carried against the ship. Similarly, to operate the launching mechanism, sometimes an electric switch is pressed, sometimes a silken cord is cut; but with either method a weight is released to fall on the trigger that is holding back the mass.

In 1934 a new launching ceremony was introduced, when two big liners were launched by wireless. On the first occasion a ship for the Holland-Africa Line was launched in a Dutch yard by General Hertzog (Prime Minister of South Africa), speaking in Pretoria. Then the Orient liner *Orion* was launched at Barrow-in-Furness, Lancashire, by the Duke of Gloucester, who was in Australia.

With their love of everything that is picturesque, the Japanese naturally take a keen interest in the ceremony and give it many touches which are typically Japanese. Over the bow of the ship that is to take the water is suspended a circular cloth cage of red and white stripes. As the ship is released this cage is ripped open and a number of song birds are freed; these birds circle round the ship as she goes down the launching ways. The belief is that the birds, in gratitude for their liberty, will always take an interest in the ship and guide her to safety in times of peril.

"Goodbye on the Mersey", by the French painter James Tissot. Starting out as a society painter in Paris, Tissot then moved to London where he lived in some style. Fashionable women were a favourite subject and later, perhaps inspired by Whistler, he produced numerous studies of the Thames.

Sometimes, but not always, flowers and flower petals are enclosed with the song birds in the cage, the petals falling over the launching party in a cloud as the cloth is ripped. The ceremony is generally preceded by a short religious service.

In Europe the Latin peoples have, perhaps, the greatest inclination to add picturesque touches to the launching ceremony. Italian shipbuilders like to complete the ship on the launching ways instead of sending her round to the fitting-out basin afterwards. This is because the Mediterranean is tideless and the ship can be launched direct into the open sea. The fitting-out basin may be some distance away in the harbour. This method is occasionally adopted also in France and other countries; provided that she is not too big, there is no technical difficulty in this. It certainly affords the spectators a thrill to see the completed ship go down with her funnels smoking and whistle blowing, to start her screw and then steam off immediately on her trials.

Chinese launches are less artistic than Japanese, but they are certainly impressive. All round the ship incense is burned to propitiate the gods. Every spectator is provided with fireworks. He is expected to make the greatest possible noise with them as well as with drums or tom-toms and with his voice. The idea of this is to frighten off devils who would otherwise remain with the ship until they brought her to disaster.

Superstition with launches is not, however, confined to the Chinese. On the North-East Coast of Great Britain it is considered most unlucky to launch a ship on a Friday. In that area, from the beginning of the shipbuilding industry until the boom days of the war of 1914-18, when the steady supply of new ships had to come before any other considerations, no instance was known of its having been risked. Even to-day launching on a Friday is avoided where possible. Experienced shipyard workers will shake their heads and quote dozens of instances of ships whose owners braved the superstition and either came to grief immediately or were unlucky throughout their lives.

This same area of hard-headed men is more prejudiced than any other district against a man acting as sponsor. It can point to innumerable examples to justify the feeling. As recently as 1928, Mr. Lund, a Norwegian shipowner, told the guests at a launching ceremony that during the war of 1914-18 he had sent a number of ships into the water christened by men or else unchristened. Not one of those ships had survived; nearly every one had had the worst of luck, until she had finally come to grief.

Another superstition which has never had much hold on official minds in the Navy, and which is rapidly dying out, is that the worst of luck will follow the ship whose name is divulged before the ceremony. Nowadays, the names of all warships, and of at least two merchantmen out of three, are well known long before the christening ceremony. But in the days of the old racing clippers such premature revelation would have been regarded as foolhardy. Recently the Cunard White Star Line, with so much at stake, kept the name of the R.M.S. *Queen Mary* a secret until her Majesty Queen Mary pronounced the christening formula.

It is considered most unlucky if the sponsor fails to break the bottle at the first attempt, and a ship is held to be practically doomed if she enters the water with the bottle still intact.

When H.M. battleship *Albion* was launched at the Thames Ironworks in 1896, by Her Majesty Queen Mary, then Duchess of York, one of the principal officials of the shipyard was an enthusiastic teetotaller and, either by his orders or from a desire to please him, the champagne had been emptied out of the bottle and water substituted. To hide the deception, the bottle was swathed with decorative ribbon until it had a thick padding. Three times the Duchess threw the bottle, three times it bounced off the steel bow. In despair, she handed it to a male spectator standing by. He tore off the ribbon, revealing the imposture and finally, managed to smash the bottle just as the ship was moving out of range. Immediately afterwards fifty people were drowned when the backwash from the ship's displacement carried away a crowded staging.

Allied to superstition is custom, and that exists in full measure in every shipbuilding district. Among the innumerable customs, logical and illogical, that were formerly always observed by Clyde shipbuilders were certain acknowledged relaxations of discipline and shipyard routine.

When a wooden ship was launched it was customary for the young carpenters and shipwrights' apprentices to conceal themselves on board, as far forward as possible. Immediately she started down the ways they emerged to secure the ribbons and rosettes that were left hanging. These were much prized by the Scottish girls in the shipbuilding districts. Another custom, which was not appreciated nearly so much by the youngsters, was for all the apprentices who could be secured to receive a sound thrashing or ducking from the older hands. The justification was that if the apprentices were not doing anything wrong at that particular moment, they had been or soon would be misbehaving.

Ceremonies, superstitions and customs go so far back into the mists of history that it is impossible to trace their origin. The ancient Mediterranean warships took the water garlanded with flowers, but often enough human sacrifices were offered to Neptune at the same time. At the launch of the Viking long-ships prisoners of war were sacrificed, but goats were later substituted. Our forefathers' customs were not always pleasant, but they indicate the importance which was attached to the launching ceremony.

Perhaps the most picturesque ceremony was in Tudor days, when the Navy was beginning to acquire popularity. In those days the ship took the water without any ceremony, but as soon as she had been secured alongside the quay, or fitting-out berth, the contemporary taste for pageantry was given full scope. The King's representative, generally the Lieutenant of the County, attended by his drummers and trumpeters, would board the ship as soon as she was tied up.

To the usual fanfares he marched round the poop, acknowledging the cheers of the spectators. He then seated himself on a decorated chair. Before this was a pedestal on which rested a silver goblet of wine. Giving the ship her name and wishing her God-speed the Lieutenant drank to the health of the ship, spilt a little wine on the deck at the four cardinal points of the compass, drank again to the health of the King, then threw the cup, with what wine remained, over the side into the water as an offering to Neptune.

This was a picturesque ceremony, but it was only to be expected that there would be somebody in authority who strongly objected to its extravagance. So the master shipwrights secretly stretched a net under the water alongside the ship and salved the goblet as soon as the excitement was over. When the courtiers at the Stuart Courts were more needy, there arose an open quarrel between the King's Lieutenants and the master shipwrights about the reversion of the goblet. This brought the whole ceremony into disrepute and led to its abandonment; but it was restored by Charles II with the custom regularized. The goblet was presented to the master builder as his acknowledged perquisite.

The Chusan Ball and Supper in celebration of the arrival of the first Royal Mail steamships from Great Britain in Australia. The Chusan are a cluster of islands at the entrance of Hang Chow Bay, south of Shanghai. P.& O., the ship's owners, carried mails to Australia, India and the Far East.

This picturesque old custom was gradually abandoned as being out of keeping with the spirit of the age. For some time there appears to have been no regular launching or christening ceremony at all.

Just when the use of a bottle of wine was begun cannot definitely be discovered, but the custom was apparently due to the efforts of the shipyard workers themselves, without any encouragement or co-operation from the authorities. They loved the ship that they had built, as good craftsmen will, and they were not satisfied to see her start her life with no better ceremony than the signing of a document in Whitehall.

Gradually the Admiralty began to appreciate the virtue of a little ceremony and, where the King's ships were concerned, made it official. About 1810 there began the custom of asking a lady to perform the christening ceremony. This has been practically universal ever since. One of the earliest instances was particularly unfortunate. A Royal Princess was invited to break the bottle over the bows of a new ship that was to be launched at Plymouth Dockyard. She missed the ship altogether, but the bottle landed on the head of a spectator standing beside the ways, doing him serious injury, for which he later obtained compensation through the courts.

Ever since then the Admiralty has taken the precaution of making the bottle fast to the bow of the ship by a piece of ribbon. In dockyard launches the bottom of the bottle is generally filled with lead to ensure that it breaks.

Wine is the traditional christening medium of the ship, but its quality may vary. "Old Hall" of Aberdeen, builder of some of the finest clipper ships, would invariably send his office boy to a certain grocer's shop on the morning of the launch, with instructions to buy a shilling bottle of "christening wine" of champagne character. He would always make a joke of this exhibition of parsimony.

On the other hand, there are many shipowners who maintain that the best of wine is not too good for the vessel that is to carry their fortune. Many owners who object to alcohol on principle have used water. Then the workers shake their heads and say that the ship cannot possibly have any luck. (There are many instances of water-christened ships which have had trouble.)

Where the owner is teetotal, water can be respected, and perhaps there was an excuse for ginger wine in American launches when the prohibition law made the use of wine illegal. But some substitutes ridicule the traditional ceremony. In 1927 a ship launched on the Clyde was christened by having a coconut broken over her bows. In the United States one American ship was launched with ice cream. Another American ship, the *Mary Earl*, intended for the molasses trade, was christened with treacle.

Nowadays a religious ceremony is part of the launching of every ship of any importance. In Roman Catholic countries it has never been abandoned. The sacrifices made by the Romans and Vikings were made with a religious object. In his diary of the year 1676, Henry Teonge, a chaplain in H.M. Fleet, describes the launch of a new galley for the Knights of Malta when his ship was visiting the island. The ceremony began with two hours of hymns and anthems, after which two priests went on board and laid their hands in benediction on every mast and major fitting, sprinkling holy water and finishing up with a public blessing. There is no doubt that the reverend diarist was impressed in spite of himself. He came from an inland parish and apparently did not know that in his own country the religious ceremony had been an integral part of the launch of the ship during the Commonwealth, although it was stopped in the early days of the Restoration. The ceremony did not return until 1875, when two parties used their influence. One was Admiral King-Hall at Devonport Dockyard, though his influence secured him no more than permission to have a short religious ceremony at the launch of the dockyard tug *Perseverance*. The other was the Princess of Wales, later Queen Alexandra, who secured a full religious ceremony, conducted by Dr. Tait, then Archbishop of Canterbury, at the launch of the ironclad battleship *Alexandra*. The full choral

service was introduced at the launch of the cruiser *Gladiator* in 1896.

Immediately after the ship has taken the water, the company generally goes into the mould loft, the biggest room in the shipyard, and sits down to a banquet lunch. In the evening the workmen have their own celebration, usually described as a "ball". After the lunch there is an excellent opportunity for happy speeches and the general passing of compliments, so that the visitors go away thoroughly satisfied with a charming ceremony. Visitors are not allowed to see anything of the anxiety which accompanies every launch. The fact that accidents happen so seldom is a tribute to the careful manner in which everything is prepared and the efficiency of all hands; but the possibility is always there.

The ship is built on a slipway leading down from the shipyard into the water, known as the permanent ways, standing ways or ground ways. When she is ready for the launch a cradle is built under her, generally called the sliding ways. Between this and the permanent ways, tallow, soft soap and oil are placed as a lubricant. Unfortunately, this lubricant may freeze in cold weather and act as a brake instead.

The cradle is built up under the bow and stern into heavy "poppets", the bow especially having to stand a tremendous strain. The cutting of the cord by the sponsor, or the pressing of an electric button, knocks away the dog-shores holding the cradle, but which are generally supported by mechanically operated holding and releasing triggers. With a push of a few feet from a ram fixed under the bow of the ship, she starts towards the water, and the next fifty or sixty seconds are as many minutes to those responsible for the launch.

HER MAJESTY AND THE SEA
The Queen, 1936

If the Queen accepts the invitation to go on board the new *Queen Mary* on one of her trial trips, it will be a signal mark of royal favour to the mammoth liner, for it is no secret that the Queen does not like sea travel. She was very young when she first accompanied her parents to Italy, and it is said that it was the rough voyage to Genoa which made the Queen ever afterwards somewhat dread a sea voyage. It is a matter of comment in British royal circles that nearly every time she has crossed the Channel the Queen has encountered stormy seas!

Her first ocean voyage was on the *Ophir* when she accompanied the King, then Duke of York, on his memorable Empire tour of 1902. Neither the outward or homeward voyages, except wonderful visits ashore, are particularly pleasant memories for the Queen. She is, frankly, not a good sailor, and the narrow confines of even a modern ship make her uncomfortable.

She likes seafarers, for the King, of course, is passionately fond of ships, but, despite all efforts, the King has never been able to interest the Queen much even in yachting. Her Majesty's open preference for shipping tours and private visits during Cowes Week in place of sailing is well known, and only on very calm and sunny days will she go afloat.

It was really not until recent years that she enjoyed the seaside. All her life she has

The Royal Yacht *Victoria and Albert III* makes her entrance into Belfast, passing Harland and Wolff's shipyard on the left. Launched in 1899, rumours percolated that the vessel was unstable and Queen Victoria never set foot aboard. Unsuitable for trans-oceanic voyages, the yacht appeared at the Coronation Review for George VI in 1937 and some of her furniture survives today aboard the *Brittania*.

29

preferred the town and the country. The Royal yacht, *Victoria and Albert,* would be much more in commission was it not for the Queen's lack of enthusiasm for the sea. She has made two voyages with the King to India, the first in 1905 and the last in 1911. The outward voyage on the last trip for the famous Delhi Durbar was rather rough, and the Queen's health suffered accordingly. On arrival at Bombay, the Queen's health recovered, but she confessed she was relieved that the trip was over.

The homeward voyage was a little smoother until home waters were reached, but the Queen this time was more accustomed to "roll".

In the interior decoration of ships the Queen takes a great interest. It is rumoured that she has made many practical suggestions for the *Queen Mary.* The story, current in America, that the Queen will travel on the ship when it makes it first trip to New York, however, can be heavily discounted. The Queen has never been in the United States, and even if she could spare the time the thought of the Atlantic rollers would, in all probability, deter her.

Curiously enough, the Queen, an inveterate reader, cannot concentrate on reading while at sea, and this is another factor which weighs heavily in the balance against sea travel. During her Empire tour, and visits to India, she took with her a big library for the voyage, but felt disinclined to open any of the volumes. Photography and sketching are her favourite recreations while at sea, and she has a large number of sea and ship photographs.

The Queen has never been a passenger on one of the great modern liners, and it may be if she boards the *Queen Mary* her prejudice against sea voyages may be modified. The Princess Royal inherits her mother's trepidity in this respect, but recently she has found her health so improved by sea trips that she is becoming a much more enthusiastic sailor.

The Queen cannot be described as an ardent cat-lover, and she has a superstitious dread of encountering a cat of any colour as she embarks or leaves a ship. Once in the *Ophir,* while sitting in a sequestered place on one of the decks, a cat refused to leave her chair. The Queen summoned a passing sailor

and asked him to remove it. The animal jumped out of the man's arms, however, right into the sea. The Queen was much upset, but, fortunately, it was no bad omen.

While at sea the Queen eats sparingly, and enjoys fruit most of all. When sailing to India in 1911, she ate no meat dishes at all, and lost a great deal of weight. The Queen, like the Prince of Wales, has a horror of stoutness, and she laughingly says that she finds sea travel the best antidote!

Rather oddly, the Queen has a partiality for sea stories. Thanks to the King, she knows a great deal about the Navy, and also the mercantile marine. The King believes in the old sailor saying, that "no true hearted sailor's wife ever loved the sea". It is known, however, that the Queen regrets her inability to enjoy life on the "ocean wave". That she has travelled so much by sea is one more proof of her high conception of public service.

The *Queen Mary,* named after her, is the last word in ship construction, and who knows, but she may succeed in banishing the dread of sea travel from the mind of the Queen, after whom she is named.

WHERE THE QUEEN MARY WAS BUILT
Frank C. Bowen

Famous for having built ocean greyhounds, John Brown's yard at Clydebank reached the peak of its achievements with the construction of the Cunard White Star R.M.S. *Queen Mary.*

The present firm of John Brown & Co. is a combination of John Brown's steel interests from Sheffield and J. & G. Thomson's shipbuilding and engineering works on the Clyde. Thomson's were closely associated with the Cunard Company, for which they built such ships as the *Bothnia* (4,535 tons) of 1874 and *Gallia* (4,809 tons) of 1879. At that time, however, the Cunard had for some years lost their interest in the Atlantic Blue Riband, and it was on the Cape trade, with the Union Liner *Moor,* that Thomson's first came into real prominence for speed. Their first Blue Riband was gained with the National Liner *America.*

She was laid down in 1883, a beautiful clipper-stemmed steamer of 5,528 tons which won the record in 1884.

Towards the end of the 'eighties, when the British Government was willing to support the construction of bigger and faster Atlantic liners to have them as a reserve of cruisers in wartime, the Inman Line went to them for the *City of New York* and the *City of Paris*. These were ships of 10,500 tons apiece, designed as rivals to the White Star *Teutonic* and *Majestic*, of approximately the same size and speed. The competition between these four ships was intensely keen and took the speed of the Atlantic record to over twenty knots for the first time; but in the early 'nineties the American shareholders in the Inman Line secured the transfer of the company to America as the American Line, and the *City of New York* and the *City of Paris* became the *New York* and *Philadelphia*, famous in both war and peace.

In 1899, John Brown & Co. of Sheffield were looking out for a shipyard to combine with their steel business and chose that of J. & G.

Top. "The Big Four" from the White Star Line were amongst the most successful ships on the Western ocean and, for a time, the largest liners afloat. The *Celtic* was commissioned in 1901 and her sister, the *Cedric*, delivered in 1903. Their success was followed by two larger ships, the *Baltic* and the *Adriatic*.

Centre. The incomplete *Bismarck*, ordered by the Hamburg–American Line shortly before World War I, was ceded as war reparations and sailed as the *Majestic* (1922), the largest ship afloat until the appearance of the French *Normandie* (1935).

31

The White Star *Teutonic*, by William L. Wyllie. Seen at Spithead in 1899 and centrepiece of the naval review, the liner was much admired by Kaiser Wilhelm II – a valuable advertisement for White Star. The Admiralty, determined to have a regular arrangement with the shipowners, offered them a subsidy for liners to double as armed merchant cruisers in time of war and White Star were the first to take advantage of the scheme.

Thomson after having examined almost every establishment that was likely to be sold for the very good price that they were willing to offer.

The change of ownership made no difference to the yard's policy, except that it gave it bigger resources for expansion. The Cunard *Saxonia* (14,281 tons) of 1900 was designed for the greatest comfort and had a splendid reputation for steadiness. She was followed, among many other ships, by the Cunarders *Carmania* and *Caronia* of 1905 – "The Pretty Sisters" – which were of over 20,000 tons each and which, while they did not aspire to high speed, were of the greatest interest technically, as the *Carmania* was the first New York liner to be fitted with turbine engines and led the way directly to the construction of the *Lusitania*.

When the Government decided to assist the Cunard Line in the building of the 25-knot *Lusitania* and *Mauretania*, each with a gross tonnage of over 30,000, there were not many ship-builders who were willing to take such a risk and to spend the amount of money that was necessary for their safe construction. John Brown's had the contract for the *Lusitania*, and

to permit her launch expensive dredging operations were also necessary. The ship was an unqualified success, recapturing the Blue Riband after it had been held by the Germans for ten years, and was a great popular favourite until she was sunk by a torpedo on May 7, 1915.

In 1914 the Cunard Company wanted a third ship to supplement the *Lusitania* and *Mauretania*, but for her they had no Government assistance and thus they had to design her entirely as a commercial proposition. This ship was the *Aquitania*, and her speed was, therefore, slightly less than that of her two consorts, and her gross tonnage had to be increased to over 45,000, so that her cargo and passenger accommodation should be increased. Like the *Lusitania*, she was a ship with a very definite personality, such as the Clydesiders dearly love, and on service she proved a popular and profitable ship.

Since the war of 1914-1918 John Brown's have built a large number of liners of all types and sizes, both steam and motor. When the Cunard Company, as it was then, approached the ship-builders for the construction of the *Queen Mary* in 1930, John Brown's were one of the very few yards in the country capable of tackling such a colossal task, and the price that they quoted was well below that of rival concerns. Also, they were willing to contract for the whole ship; some of the other builders fought shy of such huge commitments, so that John Brown's got the order and proceeded with the construction of the ship. In the meantime they built the Canadian Pacific *Empress of Britain* (42,348 tons), which holds the Canadian record and which is one of the most noteworthy ships under the British flag.

The advantage of the steady supply in a big contract, especially when it has to be carried out against time, is obvious, but the company also gained immensely by supplying so much of its own material.

There are eight slips for the construction of ships, the biggest capable of taking a vessel of no fewer than 1,000 feet in length. Five of these are in the East, or Main, Yard and the three other slips in the West, two of the three

The Needles Channel leads into the Solent. Pilot vessels cruise in the vicinity of the Needles outside the channel and, in bad weather, inside the channel. The Needles, dangerous isolated rocks on the west coast of the Isle of Wight, are marked by a lighthouse.

being covered in. The slipway in the East Yard, on which the *Queen Mary* was built, had to be extended to take her full length in safety, and millions of cubic yards of earth were removed for the purpose. The foundations were reinforced, so that there should be no chance of their failing under the enormous weight that was put on the slip. When the construction of the ship was held up for many months, it was quite generally believed that she had sunk considerably, as she might be expected to do in such circumstances, but she was not distorted by one inch, and this aspect has impressed technicians abroad more, perhaps, than any other. The yard has a frontage on to the River Clyde of over 1,000 yards, situated on the north bank of the river, directly opposite the point at which the tributary Cart runs into it. This offers

additional water for the launch of an exceptionally large ship, and when the *Queen Mary* was to come off the slip, the tributary was dredged considerably in order to ensure absolute safety.

The building slips, with their elaborate equipment are backed by numerous shops of all kinds and the firm is one of the very few private concerns in Great Britain to maintain its own experimental tank. This was installed in 1903, is carefully placed to obtain the maximum results, and has water and dry docks at either end for trimming the models. The elaborate plant necessary for making the wax models to the required precision is grouped round the docks; the towing carriage and all necessary auxiliaries are electrically driven. This tank is 400 feet long by 20 feet wide, and in it sixteen models of the *Queen Mary* made over 4,000 trials.

33

A GREAT SHIP SAILS
E. Burnand Mount

"For New York left Southampton." This is the brief announcement of a liner's departure. But before sailing day arrives organizations are at work to prepare for a voyage that may take six days or six weeks.

For the individual passenger, his embarkation in a giant liner may be a notable event. The voyage may open a new epoch, holding the promise of adventure and romance. Yet the beginning of an ocean voyage is the reverse of dramatic. It is as matter-of-fact and as easy, so far as the passenger is concerned, as boarding an omnibus. Armed with tickets and passport, he travels in a comfortable boat train, walks to a barrier where his papers are quickly examined, and goes aboard. Later a few concise orders are passed to all concerned, the ship's siren blows, and she is under way. The great adventure has begun as easily as that.

The real drama of sailing day lies in the complex preparations that are necessary, and in the organization which completes them so smoothly. A ship's company is faced with a passage of days – or sometimes of weeks – during which it must be completely self-supporting. To achieve this, much must be done in advance. Let us examine the work of the quayside, taking for an example a great transatlantic liner, such as the *Aquitania*, the *Bremen* or the *Normandie*. These are some of the largest vessels afloat and thus present the greatest sailing problems.

A ship is routinely stripped of personnel and contents after each voyage. As soon as she docks from one voyage, she must be prepared for the next. The work begins with the signing-off and paying-off of all the crew, and their re-engagement for the next voyage. The captain himself heads the list, signing a fresh agreement before each sailing. This is his first act upon docking. Immediately he sets about new preparations. He visits the Custom House, completes the formality of entering the ship's arrival, and signs the papers for the outward voyage.

Various official departments are concerned with the sailing of a ship: the Board of Trade, the Board of Customs and Excise, the Port Sanitary Authority, the Immigration Department of the Home Office (which deals also with emigration), Trinity House (or some other body), which supplies pilotage, and, of course, the Port Authority. Officials from these departments visit the ship constantly during preparations.

The paying-off of the crew is under the management of the owners' Shipping Department, and is attended by Board of Trade officials. Generally most members of a passenger liner's crew sign on at once for the next voyage and receive the official embarkation pass to join the ship on the day before sailing; any new members of the crew are also signed on then. Under the Merchant Shipping Acts a ship's company must be maintained at a regulation strength. This quota having been reached, the Board of Trade officials issue a form (Form AA) which is necessary before the Custom House "clearance" can be granted.

From the Board of Trade and from the Admiralty come the urgent Notices to Mariners. These contain detailed information of any alterations in navigation rules, or in the positions of buoys, lights and channels. For instance, the entrance to Southampton Harbour, between Cowes Roads and Southampton Water, is an S-shaped channel which is continually dredged and continually shifting because of the set of the tides. Up-to-date information about such alterations is supplied in the current Notice to Mariners.

Any ship carrying over fifty third-class passengers is defined as an "emigrant ship"; so this term applies to a transatlantic liner. Board of Trade officials attend a muster of the whole crew of an emigrant ship on the day before sailing. At this the complete boat-drill, fire-drill and bulkhead-door-drill are performed. The drills are repeated early the next morning, this time with the crew equipped with life-belts.

Another safety-measure consists in the Plimsoll-line (load-line or freeboard) regulations, and it is the duty of the Board of

"Dunottar Castle", by Sir F.W. Brangwyn. Brangwyn later became known as a painter of murals and produced murals for the *Salles Jacques Cartier* on the *Empress of Britain.* An official war artist in World War I, Brangwyn enjoyed a higher reputation in Europe than in England.

Dunottar Castle, **the first ship of the Castle Line to carry mails from Southampton to Cape Town in 1891, seen in Phaleron Bay. Carrying yards on her foremast and barquentine rigged, she was very much a descendant from the days of sail.**

Trade to ensure that these are observed. To carry out this duty the Board of Trade may use one of two methods: a report from its own surveyors, or a report from one of the "Classification Societies". The principal classification societies, so far as British ships are concerned, are three in number, and have been set up with the initial purpose of classifying ships for insurance. The best-known is Lloyd's Register of Shipping, generally known as Lloyd's Register. The other two are the British Corporation and the British Committee of Bureau Veritas. The Board of Trade has its own large survey staff; and, by using existing organizations also, is saved the great cost of maintaining a staff of surveyors sufficient to cope with every ship sailing from British ports.

Bond of £2,000

Upon receipt of the report that the load-line (Plimsoll-line) regulations have been fulfilled the Board of Trade issues its load-line certificate. This must by law be exhibited in the ship.

Another Board of Trade form which must be completed for emigrant ships is "Survey 47A". This covers what is known as the "continuing bond". The owners and the master of every emigrant ship lodge a bond of £2,000 with the Crown to ensure that certain provisions of the Merchant Shipping Acts shall be observed.

The provisions ensured by the £2,000 penalty in the bond include that "the ship shall at the time of her departure be in all respects seaworthy"; that "throughout the voyage at least four quarts of pure water shall be allowed daily to each steerage passenger"; and that "any engagement made at the beginning of a voyage to call at an intermediate port for fresh water shall be fulfilled".

This is known as a continuing bond, so called because it is considered sufficient for each successive master to endorse the original bond. Its completion is generally entrusted to the Chief Customs Officer of the port – another instance of using the existing organization in preference to setting up a new one. The final form to be completed before the

ship sails is the Board of Trade "Survey 32". This form, duly signed by the Emigration Officer, is a Certificate of Clearance which contains complete information as to the ship's itinerary, details of the passengers in each class, and of the crew; "Survey 32" also gives details of the total numbers aboard, the amount of "clear" space, and the number of beds.

The department next in importance to the Board of Trade is the Board of Customs and Excise. Returns must be made to the Customs officers of dutiable supplies, such as food, drink, and tobacco, which the chief steward may wish to take aboard the ship. As they are for consumption afloat, these escape excise duty and so must be withdrawn from a bonded warehouse, where they are loaded under arrangements made by the Customs authorities. The appropriate returns are accompanied by a request for the release of such goods, or for their supply by various firms direct, free of duty. Once the supplies are aboard, a "Victualling Bill" must be filled out, giving detailed particulars of the dutiable goods taken aboard. The customs officials must also receive from the captain a return of the total amount of dutiable goods which it is intended to carry as stores or cargo. A declaration of the total number of passengers outward bound from British ports is required also.

On another form, oddly entitled "Entry Outwards", the Board of Customs and Excise requires a report of the inward cargo still remaining on board, and a certificate of the exact position of the load-line above water. This supplies a quick and easily ascertained check against extensive smuggling, where a smaller

ship is concerned, should the vessel call at another port in the United Kingdom.

The next department to be considered is the Port Sanitary Authority. The Port Medical Officer attends the muster of the crew, passing them as fit. He looks especially for symptoms of virulent infectious diseases such as typhus, smallpox and cholera, and will if necessary, prohibit any one, crew or passenger, from sailing. Satisfied with both crew and passengers, he issues his Bill of Health.

The Immigration Department of the Home Office is represented at the quayside on sailing day. It is the duty of its officials to examine the papers of outward-bound passengers. It may happen that they are also ensuring the departure of an unwanted alien who is being deported from Great Britain.

The Port Authority officials must be satisfied, before a ship sails, that all her port dues have been paid; and they are consulted as to the exact time for sailing. Their chief executive on the quayside is the Dock or Harbour-Master. In some ports they are the owners of the tugs, and then arrangements for tugs must be made with them.

Trinity House is the body controlling outside pilots in British waters, i.e. those outside rivers and ports. It is to this organization that application must be made for a pilot who will navigate the ship through coastal waters. The coastal waters are nowadays covered by the "choice" pilot who will handle the ship in compulsory waters.

These official measures taken by law to ensure the safety and health of the passengers and crew are administered efficiently and with a minimum of officialdom. For about ships there is that which promotes comradeship, co-operation and easy running.

While the ship is in dock, the Marine Superintendent is virtually her captain. He takes over as soon as the first hawser is made fast and relinquishes his responsibility only when the last hawser is cast off. Under his supervision all the papers are handled and passed through – refitting, refuelling, repairing and replenishment of stores are all carried out by the various departments under his

authority. His work, well done, ensures that the ship about to sail is "in all respects seaworthy". There is so much detail, and so little time for hitches.

The Marine Superintendent's office – known also as the Shipping Department – is responsible for the co-ordination of all this work. His staff plans and organizes the routine of paying-off and signing-on the crew. The Cunard White Star Company reckons to handle a crew of 1,000 men in an hour. The safety drills and inspection of the men by Board of Trade officials and by the doctor are under the Marine Superintendent's direct control. He arranges also all the work to be done on the hull of the ship (as distinct from that done by the Engineering and Furnishing Departments, which carry out their own tasks).

He directs the taking aboard of thousands of tons of fresh water and oil fuel. External painting and cleaning are in the hands of his department. The ship's boats must be inspected, and necessary repairs carried out. Deck gear must be overhauled, navigational instruments and gear must be tested. Their efficiency depends on the Marine Superintendent's thoroughness. Time of departure is arranged by him, and he engages the tugs and pilots. This work is over only when the last hawsers are cast off and the great liner is under way.

Meanwhile the other departments are ceaselessly at work on their own tasks. The Furnishing Department – its exact name varies in different companies – must first of all attend to the laundering of all soiled linen. Although many great liners have their own laundries aboard, these can by no means handle the whole volume of linen used during a six-days' voyage. For example, every passenger has two clean towels a day – if the passenger list numbers 2,000 and the voyage is of six days, 24,000 towels are required. Indeed it is not exceptional for the Furnishing Department to take 100,000 pieces of linen, attend to their laundering and return them to the ship within forty-eight hours. All this linen must be checked as it goes ashore and checked again when it is returned. The work is undertaken by selected stewards from the ship.

The Furnishing Department, too, is responsible for all the furniture, carpets, linoleum, tapestries, curtains, hangings and pictures in the ship. The floor coverings alone may cover many acres. The interior decoration is in this department's hands. Every time a ship docks, some repainting of the passengers' quarters is carried out; and every square inch is thoroughly cleaned. Yet not a painter, carpenter or joiner will be visible on sailing day. There is a rigid rule that all work must be finished before the passengers come aboard, and it goes ill with the department if the rule is broken.

Below decks, in the engine-room, there is immense activity. The greatest task machinery is called upon to do across the Atlantic is to propel a vessel of many thousand tons, for 3,000 miles, and for six days without stopping. Other forms of transport all have their breathing spaces, but a ship's power must not fail her. The Engineering Department must see that the vast motive power of the ship is unimpaired. The engineers first examine the main propelling machinery, which may develop between 15,000 and 150,000 horse-power. If signs of weakness are disclosed, the faulty parts must be replaced, tested and approved in the short time available. Then refuelling must be done. This is a less arduous business than in the old days of coal-burning. To-day an oil tanker or oil barges come alongside; working at full pressure, they can pump 7,000 or 8,000 tons of oil into the tanks in a little over twelve hours.

The Problem of Stores

When coal was used, hundreds of men took days to carry aboard from barges the baskets of coal and empty them down the coal-ports in the ship's side. The resultant clean-up was a stupendous task in itself; coal dust seemed to penetrate everywhere. As well as the main engines and boilers, there is a mass of auxiliary machinery to be tested. Special machines are installed aboard a luxury liner to work the cargo derricks, anchor windlass, warping winches, steering gear, bulkhead doors, cooking machinery, refrigerating plant, heating and ventilating system, and sanitary and domestic water supplies. The Superintendent Engineer, through his staff, must ensure that all this is in first-class condition. During the voyage the engine-room crew tends the machines with expert care; but since they must work continuously, there is no opportunity for a full examination until the ship is in dock. Apart from the machines themselves, there are hundreds of miles of pipes, cables and wires which must be inspected.

Stringent Board of Trade regulations have also to be satisfied; and the Classification Societies insist on their own exacting standards on behalf of the insurance underwriters.

Great quantities of engineering stores have to be taken aboard, in addition to the fuel, oil and water, for the main engines and boilers. There may be as many as a dozen different kinds of oil used aboard the ship for lubrication, illumination and cleaning. Tool kits may have to be replenished or replaced. Cotton waste, soap, lime, and soda and carbon dioxide for the refrigerating plant, must all be supplied in sufficient quantities.

The last job of the Engineering Department – unless the ship is a motor vessel – is to see that steam is available for the machinery when the telegraph rings down "stand-by". The engines are "turned over" an hour or so before sailing, and the sirens are all tested to see they are clear.

A long blast on these same sirens at sailing hour proclaims that the Engineering Department's work is done, and that the ship is once more ready for her 3,000-miles adventure.

She sails, a complete city, self-supporting. That there shall be no lack of necessities and luxuries is the responsibility of the Catering Department, which works in conjunction with the ship's Chief Steward. His task, which resembles housekeeping on a gigantic scale, is to know the exact quantity of stores left over from the previous voyage and to calculate what he will need before the fresh voyage begins. He passes his estimates to the Superintendent Caterer, who arranges supplies. Since provision must be made for approximately 2,000 passengers and 1,000 crew, all eating three meals a day, some 9,000 meals are served daily. Thus 54,000 meals will be required during a

six-days' transatlantic crossing. And this does not take into account the mid-morning soup, afternoon tea, and the appetizing buffet-snacks which are served about eleven p.m. in the lounges. Moreover, in the first-class dining-room, the day's menus generally offer a variation of more than a hundred dishes.

Meanwhile, the kitchen equipment is inspected; utensils are repaired and replaced. A stocktaker goes over the inventory of china, glass, and earthenware, amounting to approximately 100,000 pieces, as well as 25,000 pieces of cutlery.

A Task Well Done

Thousands of empty bottles are put ashore and replaced by thousands of full ones. In addition, all dutiable stores taken aboard, eatable or drinkable, must be reported on the Victualling Bill to the Customs. All surplus stores are listed and checked.

The Freight Department is just as fully occupied. On a "quick turn-round" – as a short stay in port is termed – cargo is discharged as nearly as possible at the same time as the new cargo is loaded. All outward-bound cargo for the transatlantic liners arrives within forty-eight hours of sailing.

There are many other detailed preparations for sailing. The ship's doctor, for instance, must re-stock his dispensary. The library stewards take aboard new books, magazines and papers; they also procure a large quantity of stamps. (More than 10,000 letters have been mailed during a single voyage.) Electricians and plumbers attend to the gymnasium equipment and to the swimming pool. Wireless experts are busy in the radio room. There is even a ship's gardener, who is in charge of the thousands of plants and flowers needed for decoration.

When all the work is completed, the Marine Superintendent inspects the ship before handing over to the captain. He sees work superlatively well done; complex tasks which have been performed in the minimum time. The record "turn-round" for one of the mammoth liners at Southampton was accomplished at an incredible speed; in under twelve hours between docking and sailing. However accustomed the man in charge may be, the moment when the last gangway goes cannot fail to be a proud one – a moment filled with the sense of achievement. He and his expert staff have made that moment possible.

BRITAIN'S PREMIER PASSENGER CENTRE
Sydney Howard

Southampton is the premier port of the British Empire for the great liners. As many as seventeen of the world's largest liners have sailed from this port in one day. Southampton deals with thirty-seven per cent of the ocean passenger traffic of the United Kingdom – which means that approximately one out of every three persons who enter or leave the United Kingdom passes up or down Southampton Water.

Those five sea miles from the port of Southampton to Calshot Castle are a highway of romance. It is a highway along which men have set out and returned from hazardous enterprises, expeditions of high courage and missions of international importance. In war and peace, Southampton and the stretch of water that is a gateway of the world has played its part in history.

Great ships are neither built nor broken up at Southampton. It is their port when they are

Southern Railway Southampton Docks. The greatest increase in the growth and importance of Southampton occurred after 1892 when the docks system passed from the Southampton Dock Company to the Southern Railway (formerly the London and South Western Railway Company).

39

in the pride of their glory: and it is at Southampton that great ships are helped to keep their glory. Here is the world's largest graving dock – the King George V Graving Dock – opened by King George V in July 1933. This dock would be large enough to accommodate a vessel of 100,000 tons. It was built chiefly to accommodate the *Queen Mary*, and it is one of the world's engineering wonders.

Liners are dry-docked for regular overhauls, and, if necessary, they can be dry-docked so quickly that their dry-docking may mean only a brief pause in the liner's work.

Double tides, a local phenomenon, have added greatly to the value of the port, especially during the war of 1914-18. The period of high water lasts about two hours, during which the tidal rise and fall is negligible; the sandy clays and gravel of the channel bed form good holding ground for the anchors of ships. Landlocked as it is, with its approaches protected by the Isle of Wight and with the additional advantages of the double tides, Southampton Water is one of the finest and safest harbours in the British Isles.

The Ocean Dock was completed in 1911, and was at first called the White Star Dock, as it was intended for the big liners of that company which had decided to make Southampton its terminal port. Other great liners followed this lead, however, so the name of the dock was changed to the Ocean Dock in 1922. No fewer than five large liners can berth in the Ocean Dock at the same time.

On one notable occasion the *Mauretania* (30,696 tons), *Berengaria* (52,101 tons), *Homeric* (34,351 tons), *Majestic* (56,599 tons) and *Olympic* (46,439 tons) – making an aggregate total of 220,186 tons – were in this dock together. In addition to these wet docks – only one of which, the Inner, is non-tidal – dry docks were built. There are six in this area, the largest being the Trafalgar Dock, completed in 1905. Its construction was hurried on to meet the growing demands of German shipping, then becoming a big factor in the transatlantic trade. Southampton, by reason of its position, had a natural attraction for the German-

American traffic. When the American liners first came to the port, in 1893, they could only just get over the mud. Three years later there was a minimum depth of 30 feet.

The construction of the Extension Quay is one of the greatest engineering feats undertaken in Great Britain. A huge area had to be dredged and reclaimed before the concrete quay could be added. An untidy waste of mud-flats between two points was filled in, and the river dredged so that ships could berth. About 20,000,000 tons of silt and soil had to be shifted in the process. Furthermore, the construction of the graving dock was almost a

The Empress Dock, Southampton

superhuman task. The engineers surrounded the site with a gravel bank and made this watertight by a curtain of sheet steel driven along the centre line. They pumped out the site and began digging.

Water threatened to burst up, below the dock, but tube wells were sunk into the sand and the danger was averted. The dock holds 260,000 tons of water and can be emptied in four hours by centrifugal pumps. The steel door, which weighs 4,600 tons, was floated round to Southampton from the Tees, where it was made. This great dock, named after King George V, who opened it, is the "cot" of the

Queen Mary, in which she rested when her propellers, rudder and underwater sections were examined after her trip from the Clyde in March, 1936.

At one period in 1935 eight of the eleven merchant ships in the world with a tonnage in excess of 40,000 tons gross were making Southampton either a terminal port or a port of call. These were the *Majestic, Berengaria, Aquitania, Olympic, Empress of Britain, Bremen* and *Europa*, and the *Ile de France*. The only two other ships were the *Rex* and the *Conte di Savoia* of the Italia Line, whose route is to the Mediterranean via Gibraltar.

The *Normandie*, 86,496 tons gross, made Southampton her first port of call on her westward passage across the Atlantic after she had entered service.

An interesting development was the decision of the Red Star Line to make Southampton a port of call for the *Westernland* and the *Pennland* on the New York-Antwerp service; these liners are partly floating garages. The former third-class accommodation on three decks of these liners was converted into garages for carrying uncrated motor-cars. When the liner berths at Southampton the cars are brought from below on an electric lift to the deck and then moved to another which lowers them down the side of the ship to the quay.

ROMANCE OF THE MAURETANIA
F. E. Dean

The establishment of faster runs on the Atlantic crossing has always proved a difficult problem – for a variety of reasons. Among the chief of them is that to add even one knot to a ship's speed it is necessary to augment the engine power by an amount quite disproportionate to the increase in speed. Financial and political considerations also have to be taken into account and new difficulties have to be faced in connexion with the building of a ship large enough to accommodate the necessarily more powerful machinery.

All these problems, and more, were presented to the men responsible for one of the most remarkable ships of all time, the *Mauretania*, holder of the Atlantic record for more than twenty years and the sister of the *Lusitania*.

In 1897 the Blue Riband of the Atlantic had been won by a fine North German Lloyd steamer, the *Kaiser Wilhelm der Grosse*, of 14,350 tons gross, with 32,000-horse-power engines that gave a speed of over 22 knots. This was a speed that would take some beating, and the challenge came at a bad time in the history of British shipping. Public concern at the position was increasing. The *Etruria*, last of the Cunarders to be built with a

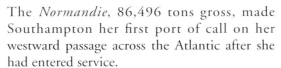

single screw, broke her propeller shaft in mid-Atlantic, and for ten days was on tow to the Azores. The Cunard Company chartered another steamer to carry passengers and mails to their destination, but again public opinion was incensed.

The Cunard Company then announced that it would lay down two steamers of 30,000 tons to recapture Great Britain's position in the Atlantic trade. The building of these two ships was to be carried out with the assistance of the Government on terms that would keep them under the British flag and provide a pair of fast auxiliary cruisers in the event of war.

These were the circumstances that governed the building of two of the most famous of all ships – the *Lusitania*, whose end stirred the whole English-speaking world to arms, and the *Mauretania*, the ship that was destined to survive storms and war and to add much to the glory of Great Britain's Mercantile Marine.

The agreement between the Cunard Company and the Government was reached in July 1903, and for two years plans were discussed, rejected and re-drafted for ships that were to be the largest and fastest in the world. Admiralty requirements had to be satisfied in the matter of possible conversion for service as auxiliary cruisers.

Accordingly a large number of experiments were carried out with models in the Government testing tanks. The models were one-forty-eighth full size, and much valuable information was obtained from them. The shipbuilders however, required even more particulars on which to base the design of the *Mauretania*, and a wooden launch was built to

a scale of one-sixteenth full size. This launch was run up and down the Northumberland Dock, on the River Tyne, and carried out hundreds of valuable experiments over a period of two years.

Then there was the all-important question of the type of machinery to be installed. The steam turbine at the beginning of the twentieth century was still in its infancy, but marine engineers had already prophesied that the new arrival would go far. Their opinion was justified; but at that period taking the decion to equip the world's largest ship with a comparatively new type of machinery needed considerable enterprise and courage.

Another innovation that was suggested but not adopted until many years afterwards was the use of oil fuel for firing the boilers. In the early years of the century, supplies of fuel oil could not be regarded as absolutely reliable, and its cost was high. The ultimate supremacy of oil firing was, however, foreseen and the bunkers and furnaces in the *Mauretania* were so built that conversion to liquid fuel was possible without undue difficulty.

For months the preparatory work went forward. Every aspect of the work was discussed and agreed upon by committees of

experts. The city of Liverpool also took a hand in preparing for the new Cunarders, and nearly 250,000 tons of material were dredged from the bed of the River Mersey alongside the famous Princes Landing Stage. New moorings were also provided in the Mersey.

Finally, on September 20, 1906, the Dowager Duchess of Roxburghe broke the traditional bottle of champagne on the stem of the giant vessel and the hull slid into the waters of the Tyne. The *Mauretania* was built by Swan, Hunter and Wigham Richardson, and was fitted with Parsons steam turbines. The gross tonnage of the *Mauretania* was 31,938. Her overall length was 790 feet, her beam 88 feet, moulded depth 60 ft. 6 in. and draught 36 ft. 3 in. The length of the promenade deck was 452 feet, and the boat deck was 584 feet long.

There were seven decks amidships and two orlop decks fore and aft. The hull was subdivided into 175 watertight compartments in addition to the protection afforded by the cellular double bottom extending to above the bilge keels. There were fifteen watertight bulkheads, and, of the watertight doors, thirty-eight could be closed from the bridge. The designed speed of the ship was 25 knots, but this was greatly exceeded on many occasions in her long life.

The turbine machinery of 68,000 shaft horse-power, was coupled direct to the four propeller shafts. Two high pressure turbines drove the two out board shafts and two low-pressure turbines drove the inboard shafts, to each of which a reverse turbine was connected for going astern. Steam was supplied by twenty-three double-ended and two single-ended boilers working at a pressure of 195 lb per sq. m.

The First Trials

The total heating surface of the boilers was 159,000 sq. ft., the grate area 4,060 sq. ft. and there were 192 furnaces into which the "black squad" were required to shovel 1,000 tons of coal a day. The bunker capacity was 6,000 tons, enough for one Atlantic crossing with an allowance for bad weather. The *Mauretania* was converted to oil firing in 1921. Turning

from the technical to the human aspect of this wonderful ship we find that her passenger accommodation makes a good showing even when compared with ships built more than a quarter of a century later. When first commissioned the Mauretania carried 563 first-class, 464 second- and 1,138 third-class passengers, in addition to a large crew, numbering some 938 officers and men.

Thirteen months after her launch the completed *Mauretania* was scheduled for her steam trials, but as she was so much a "vast experiment" her builders indulged in yet another departure from routine. Five days before she was due for the all-important official trials her engineers took her out into the North Sea. The builders wanted to make sure. With the world's largest ship, and engines of a type promising but not fully proved, they wanted to have a little private rehearsal.

Willing hands fed those roaring furnaces, and the four giant turbines hummed in harmony as the stem of the great ship clove the seas at speed for the first time. Faster and faster the quadruple screws drove the huge vessel at a speed never before attained by an ocean liner. And then the telegraph rang in the engine-room "Reduce speed". Was the huge hull distorting under the enormous strain ? No, the captain merely intimated that he was being shaken off his bridge.

A redistribution of weight cured that trouble for all time, and on October 22, 1907, the *Mauretania* left the Tyne for her official trials, which began on November 5, after Scotland had been rounded. Day and night, steaming continuously through wind and rain, the new Cunarder covered 1,216 miles at an average speed of 26.04 knots. Part of that run was accomplished at a speed of 27.36 knots.

Then followed other speed and turning tests with highly satisfactory results. With rudder hard over and all turbines full ahead, the turning circle was only three and three-quarter lengths. In the years that followed a quick turn was to save her from the death-dealing blow of a torpedo, which would otherwise have struck her below the water-line. Eleven days after her final trials the *Mauretania* left Liverpool on her

Cunard Magazine

Vᴼ L. 13. **AUGUST** 1954 Nᴼ 2.

During the twenties Cunard maintained an Express Service between Southampton and New York with the classic *Mauretania* (legendary holder of the Blue Riband), the *Aquitania* and the former German ship *Berengaria*. The service was, without question, the finest of any company.

maiden voyage to New York. The official timing of that voyage was: "Length of ocean passage, 5 days 5 hours 10 minutes. Average speed, 22.21 knots". In the preceding September the *Lusitania* had already run her maiden voyage to New York at an average speed of 23.01 knots, with a return voyage at 23.993 knots. The Blue Riband had been regained for Great Britain.

No immediate record was achieved, however, by the *Mauretania,* and with good reason. At 7.30 in the evening of Saturday, November 16, 1907, the liner left Princes Landing Stage, Liverpool and there followed a wonderfully smooth passage through the night to Queenstown, Ireland, reached at nine o'clock on Sunday morning.

Two hours later, with additional passengers and mails on board, the *Mauretania* faced the might of the Atlantic Ocean for the first time. For just one hour on that wintry Sunday the great ship gave a demonstration of her speed and then she met the weather and drove through it.

A Stokehold Inferno

Those were the days when stokeholds were infernos of blinding coal-dust, choking fumes and blistering heat. No wonder the feats of endurance performed by the "black squad" have been eulogized in picture and verse. Liverpool Irish were the boiler-room staff in the *Mauretania* – tough men for one of the toughest jobs in the world. Four hours at a time was the length of a shift, and every man worked two shifts every twenty-four hours. Trimmers plied pick and shovel in the almost unbreathable atmosphere of the bunkers – eyes, nostrils, mouth and lungs everlastingly sprayed with close-clinging coal-dust, wheeling barrow loads of coal to the firing flats ready for the stokers' shovels.

Imagine the task of just one man – feeding 5 tons of coal into a white hot furnace, each and every day. Shifts were timed by gong, prize-fight fashion, with seven-minute rounds. Seven furious minutes shooting black coal into white flame. The crash of a gong, a brief pause for breath, another gong. Then another seven minutes and the long slicers snaked in and out of furnace mouths clearing the fires of deadening clinker.

Yet another spell for raking over the incandescent mass on the fire bars and then that grim routine again and again for hours on end with floor plating turning this way and that, rising and falling with sickening movement as the mighty vessel fought storm or ocean swell. But the Irishmen from Liverpool stood up to all this. They were the finest firemen in the world, to be supplanted only by the deadly precision of the mechanical oil pump and the swirling blasts of rotary air fans.

At noon on Sunday, November 17, the *Mauretania* began her wrestle with the Atlantic rollers and by noon of the following day she had covered 571 miles of her maiden voyage. The struggle with the ocean then entered an even fiercer phase. Great seas broke over the bows, and to the man in the crow's nest aloft the great ship appeared dimly outlined below in a smother of spray, dwarfed by the gigantic seas, only the four funnel tops appearing as islands in a world of water. Picture the great stem lifting clear upwards a full 60 feet to be buried into the next mountainous sea by the mighty thrust of those giant turbines drawing hungrily on a roaring volcano of steam from battery upon battery of boilers in the depths of the great hull.

As the seas crashed on bulwark and plating the roaring avalanches of water tore at

45

everything in their path. A spare anchor, a trifle of only 10 tons, was wrenched free from the forecastle head and began to beat a devil's tattoo on the deck below it. But this was no joking matter – the smashing drive of pointed anchor flukes with 10 tons of anchor behind them was a deadly peril. Slowly the *Mauretania* turned off her course to give shelter, scant enough to the men who fought that anchor to a standstill and lashed it down.

On Tuesday at noon the log showed a run of 464 nautical miles for the twenty-four hours. On Wednesday, with improved weather, the run was 563 miles. On Thursday at noon the mileage stood at 624, a day's record and six more miles than the *Lusitania's* best for a similar period. On Friday, November 22, 1907, the *Mauretania* passed Sandy Hook. At 11.13 p.m. the liner anchored in thick fog. A deputation of influential passengers – business men in a desperate hurry for Wall Street – waited on the ship's commander, Captain John Pritchard. Would he not proceed through the fog and dock? The captain could not and would not risk a river collision and said so. Before discussion could grow cold the fog lifted, and at 6.15 p.m. the *Mauretania* docked in New York.

After a brief stay among the skyscrapers the ship turned about for England. She left New York for Liverpool at 1.35 p.m. on Saturday, November 30, and arrived in the Mersey after a run of five days 10 hours 50 minutes, at an average speed of 23.69 knots. The time on the ocean portion of the return passage was only four days 22 hours 29 minutes, and that despite fog and bad weather. One more Atlantic round voyage she made in 1907 at much the same average speeds, and then began a wonderful series of journeys during which the liner kept time with marvellous regularity.

The *Mauretania* was a hard-worked ship, and little time was allowed her for resting between voyages. Coaling was a lengthy and horribly dirty proceeding, and no light task was involved in replenishing stores. Repaintings, renewals and the repair of storm damage all took toll of her working time. But despite delays the ship made twelve round voyages in

1908. In that year she won from the *Lusitania* the Blue Riband of the Atlantic, and for more than twenty years she remained the fastest liner in the world.

She encountered her first taste of propeller trouble in May 1908, when bound for New York. One of the propellers hit submerged wreckage and a blade was torn off. With three good propellers she completed that voyage and, still in that condition, made eight more round voyages at a speed approaching her average, except for one eastward passage, which was made at only 18.72 knots.

In October 1908 the *Mauretania* was taken out of commission for her annual overhaul, and in the following January she set out for New York with a set of new propellers. These were four-bladed and cast in one piece in accordance with marine practice still in vogue. The original propellers had blades bolted on to a boss. On that January voyage westward the average speed was 23.71 knots, but on the return journey the speed rose to an average of over 25 knots, and at that level it stayed for months on end.

For the next three years the *Mauretania* ran to and fro across the Atlantic, with only a short break for her usual annual overhaul. During that period she made eighty-eight crossings, and of these seventy were runs at an average speed of over 25 knots.

Of the forty-four round voyages (Liverpool to Liverpool) no fewer than thirty-five were each completed in seventeen days, with four days in port for the "turn-round". This was a fine performance, but in addition to the high average speeds there were many instances of exceptional steaming. September in 1909 and 1910 saw westward runs at an average of 26.06 knots. In March 1910 and May 1911 the ship registered a top speed of 27 knots. Nineteen years later she was destined to average that speed for a whole Atlantic crossing.

On Active Service

So the *Mauretania* earned an unsurpassed reputation for speed and reliability. For two more years she continued to carry emigrants from Europe to the New World, business men,

Christmas Number

celebrities and tourists on their several errands. On August 1, 1914, the *Mauretania* sailed from Liverpool on her westward voyage. Four days later she received wireless instructions to make with all speed for Halifax, Nova Scotia. Great Britain had declared war on Germany. The *Mauretania* had been specially built to permit the mounting of 6-in. guns for service as an auxiliary cruiser in time of war. She continued, however, to serve the Atlantic route until October, when she was requisitioned by the Government in accordance with the Cunard Company's undertaking.

The *Mauretania,* however, was never used as an auxiliary cruiser. The use of large armed merchantmen as war vessels had been proved to be a mistake. The proof had rested largely in the fate of a German auxiliary – the famous *Kaiser Wilhelm der Grosse*, crack liner of the Atlantic in 1897. She was caught in August 1914, when coaling off Rio de Oro, on the west coast of Africa. The hunter was H.M.S. *Highflyer* an obsolete cruiser with but a tithe of the liner's speed. After a short but sharp action the *Kaiser Wilhelm der Grosse* was sunk in shallow water. It is true that the German ship had met with some success as a commerce raider, but the difficulties of coaling remained and, in any event, auxiliaries were never a match for regular warships.

47

The *Mauretania* was accordingly laid up until, with the opening of the Dardanelles campaign, an opportunity was found to use her. In May 1915, the *Mauretania* made her first voyage as a transport from Southampton, with 3,182 troops on board, bound for the Allied base of Mudros, on the island of Lemnos, in the Aegean Sea.

On May 7, 1915, her sister ship, the *Lusitania,* carrying passengers across the Atlantic to England, was torpedoed off the Old Head of Kinsale and sunk with the loss of 1,198 men, women and children.

By August 1915 the *Mauretania* had made three voyages to Mudros, carrying 10,391 officers and men. It was in the Mediterranean that the *Mauretania* came within a narrow margin of sharing the fate of her sister ship. The commander of the *Mauretania*, Captain Dow, saw the track of an approaching torpedo on the starboard bow.

Instantly the wheel was spun hard a-port. The torpedo missed by the narrow margin of about 5 feet. Calmness and quick thinking on the bridge were allied to grim courage in the confined spaces below. In engine-room and stoking flat the men stood to their jobs, crowding on all revolutions to stave off the peril that threatened all on board.

Next followed yet another transformation for the world's fastest liner. She was equipped as a hospital ship. Public rooms were turned into hospital wards packed with swing cots, and promenade and shelter decks were used as well. Three voyages the *Mauretania* made to Mudros and back, carrying 2,307 medical staff and 6,298 sick and wounded. With the evacuation of the Gallipoli peninsula the ship was paid off and her hospital equipment removed.

Once again the Cunarder became a transport, and in October and November 1916 she made two voyages from Halifax, Nova Scotia, to Liverpool, carrying 6,000 officers and men as part of Canada's contribution to the struggle on the Somme.

During the whole of 1917, Great Britain's blackest year of the war, the *Mauretania* lay up at Greenock, but early in 1918 she was again

commissioned as a transport, this time to bring American troops over to France. The work went on for seven months, steadily reinforcing the Western front with divisions from the United States. News of the war's outbreak had been flashed to the *Mauretania* on the high seas, and in the same manner she received notification of the Armistice. Thereafter followed a period when the liner's services were required to return men to their homes, and on May 27, 1919, she was finally paid off and handed back to her owners.

No war veteran, whether man or ship, was in best shape to face post-war conditions. The *Mauretania* made seven voyages on the Southampton-New York route in 1920, and ran for only four months in 1921. Her average speed was then only 18.23 knots.

Following labour troubles and difficulty in obtaining good coal, the ship's misfortunes were increased in July 1921 by an outbreak of fire that gutted all the first-class cabins on E Deck and damaged the deck above.

Conversion To Oil

That fire was a blessing in disguise, for in addition to repairing the damage the Cunard Company decided to convert the liner to an oil-burner at a cost of over £250,000. Her engines were overhauled, and by March 1922 she was back at work.

In that year the *Mauretania* made eleven round voyages across the Atlantic Ocean and twelve more in the year following. Her average speed was beginning to approach pre-war standard again. Early in 1923 she had her first experience of cruising, when for some weeks she was chartered by an American company for a trip to the Mediterranean. Thereafter followed year after year of steady work to and fro across the Atlantic with occasional cruising holidays.

In 1926 one hundred staterooms were modernized and public rooms were redecorated and refurnished. Two years later her engine room received attention. This was more than an overhaul; it was little short of a reconstruction. New condensers and pumps were installed, and improvements were made to the turbines. After this most of her voyages

were run at an average speed of over 25 knots. No queen can reign for ever, and the inevitable young rival was now due to take up the sceptre. In July 1929 the new German liner *Bremen* made the passage from Cherbourg to the Ambrose Light in four days 17 hours 42 minutes at an average speed of 27.9 knots. This was 1 knot faster than the Mauretania's best; but the gallant old ship was not to be ousted without a struggle.

On August 3, 1929, the *Mauretania* left Southampton for Cherbourg and New York with orders to do her best. Propeller revolutions varied between 205 and 210 a minute, and the engines were designed to give only 180. She did that voyage at an average speed of 26.9 knots, and her own Atlantic westbound record was broken by five hours. The *Bremen* had conquered by four hours, but the German had been favoured by the weather. For the *Mauretania* it was a defeat to be proud of. On the passage home she averaged 27.22 knots, another record voyage.

That was in 1929 and still the wonderful old ship had years of useful life ahead of her, fast passages on time with the now popular cruises at intervals. In addition to her war service the *Mauretania* made 319 voyages.

The last voyage of the famous liner, from Southampton to Rosyth, in the Firth of Forth, began on July 1, 1934.

On board the mighty *Queen Mary* there hangs a fine picture of the *Mauretania,* depicting her at Rosyth, surrounded by tugs, with the Forth Bridge as a background, and a funeral plume of black smoke rising into clouded sky.

NEW YORK – KEY TO A CONTINENT
Sidney Howard

All the world's fastest steamships services from Europe to the United States converge on the Port of New York, with its magnificent natural harbour on the Atlantic seaboard of the North American continent.

The Bush Terminal in South Brooklyn is one of the most famous terminals in the port. It is situated on the Upper Bay above the Narrows and has piers, warehouses, factories, tugs, lighters and road and railroad facilities. In New York City the goods made in the factories at the terminal are displayed to buyers, and orders are delivered from the terminal. The Atlantic and Baltic Terminals, the U.S. Army Base, and Jay Street Terminal are among the terminals on the Brooklyn shore. On the Staten Island side are the American Dock and Pouch Terminals. On the New Jersey side of the Hudson River are the numerous piers of the railway companies, and the many piers at which berth the liners and freighters of the principal companies connecting with Europe and other continents.

The increase in the size of great liners has caused many developments in the port of New York. At one time the length of the Hudson

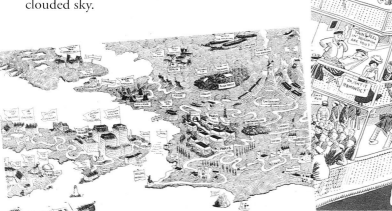

49

The correct meaning of voyage is a double-passage, out and home. Shown here are pages from a book published by Cunard.

Outward on the *Aquitania*.

Top. The Dog's Promenade on the boat deck.

Right. An Atlantic "*Rue de la Paix*", shopping in the Long Gallery.

Far right. The Aperitif Hour in the American Bar.

Right. Dancing in the Garden Lounge.

The Dogs' Promenade
'Aquitania' Boat Deck

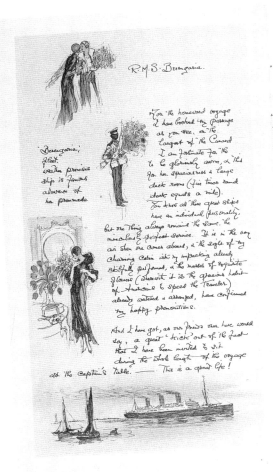

R.M.S. Berengaria.

Dinner at the Captain's Table
"Berengaria"

A Gala Dance in the
"Berengaria"

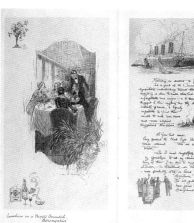

Luncheon on a Private Verandah
"Berengaria"

Homeward on the *Berengaria*.

Top. **Dinner at the Captain's table, the social centre of life aboard ship.**

Left. **The Swimming Pool.**

Far left. **A Gala dance.**

Left. **Luncheon on a Private Verandah.**

New York's famous skyline. The greatest liner piers were on the west side of Manhattan Island, facing the Hudson River. New York's waterfront, fringed with docks and served by innumerable ferries, was the busiest in the world in the Golden Age.

White Star had merged with Cunard by 1934. Regularity of performance, freedom from vibration, absence of technical troubles and economy of operation were the objectives of the Cunarders.

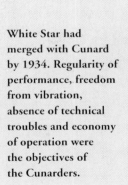

River piers on Manhattan was limited to 900 feet, but this limit has been extended to accommodate the super-liners. Piers 1,100 feet long and 125 feet wide to berth vessels such as the *Queen Mary* and the *Normandie* were provided in the Hudson River, forming the New Transatlantic Terminal. This has entailed modifying the entire pierhead line on both shores of the river, but a fairway with a width of from 2,800 feet to 3,500 feet provided at the narrowest point between the pier-heads on the New York and the New Jersey shores. At the same time the deep-water channel has been deepened and widened.

The incoming passanger is more concerned with the stupendous sky-line of New York City than with the harbour, but the harbour, with its life and movement, is one of the wonders of the world. So vast is the local traffic of ferries, tug-boats and lighters that the ocean-borne

trade is only a fraction of the total. Ferries, bridges and tunnels carry human beings and goods on, above and beneath the water which bears the argosies of the Seven Seas.

New York is the supreme port of the New World. Built on rock, the city's temperament is hard, but the port is in itself a romance. It is pre-eminently the portal to adventure and it is a city of the sea.

THE TITANIC DISASTER
Extracts from the Sphere, 1912

Crucial work was accomplished recently at the *Titanic* inquiry in plotting out of the danger area. The Attorney-General put it to the court that five vessels sent messages to the *Titanic*. These messages were as follows: *Californian*, 7.30 Sunday – Reported having sighted three large bergs five miles southward while in 42.30 N. 49.9 W. *Mesaba* – Reported seeing large heavy pack ice and great number of large bergs, also field ice, in 42 N. to 41.25 N. – 49 W. to 50.30 W. Weather good and clear. *Caronia*, nine a.m. Sunday – West-bound steamers report bergs and growlers and field ice in 42 N. 49.51 W. *America*, Sunday, 11.45 a.m (New York time) – Passed two large icebergs in 49.9 W. to 50.20 W. on outward southern track. *Baltic*, 300 miles S.E.– Reported one o'clock Sunday afternoon; number of steamships have passed icebergs between 49.9 W. – 50.20 W. on outward southern track.

The President on the Fatal Oblong

President: To sum it up, if the messages were received and were in the terms which have been stated by the Solicitor-General, this steamer was steaming her course through an oblong space having received warning that there were icebergs on the north track and the south track. She steamed through it for some time until she met her doom.

Witness: I suppose she must have done.

President: Of course the whole thing is assumption at present. In fact we have not had some of these messages proved. Can you give me any explanation of why such navigation should exist?

Witness: I don't think we had these messages.

President: Well I am asking you to assume it. I have said they have not been proved yet but we are told they are going to be. Assuming that they are can you explain how The *Titanic* was allowed to find her way into such a region?

Witness: I cannot, sir.

The Two Men in the Crow's Nest

Two men are constantly on watch day and night in the crow's nest, and when in confined waters, for example, when the ship is leaving or entering port, there may be three or four. Situated in a large liner such as the *Titanic*, some 125 ft. from the bridge, the men in the crow's nest are provided with marine telephones and speaking tubes connecting them with the wheelhouse. Fixed by a bracket to the mast is the bell, which is struck every half-hour to signify "All's well" and that the look-out men are alert. At night the bell is sometimes used to signal the bridge when a light is seen. One clang signifies that the approaching vessel is away to port, two to starboard, and three dead ahead. The men are on watch in the nest for four hours' duration, excepting the dog watch, and are usually specially trained and required to pass an eyesight test.

The *Titanic* inquiry was resumed at Westminster under the presidency of Lord Mersey. The principal witness on Tuesday was Mr. Bruce Ismay, who was examined by the Attorney-General. He said he was managing director of the Oceanic Steam Navigation Company, Ltd., which owned the *Titanic*. The share capital of that company was held by the International Mercantile Company of America.

Lord Mersey: "How many British companies does the American Trust control?"

Mr. Ismay: "Five."

"And how many American companies?" – "Two."

The Attorney-General: "There was no slowing down after ice was reported?" – "No."

"You knew the proximity of ice was a danger?" – "There is always more or less danger with ice."

"You knew you would be in the region of ice that night?" – "I believed so."

Answering further questions about the ice message Mr. Ismay told the Attorney-General, "The captain is responsible for the navigation of the ship."

53

The Attorney-General: "You were the managing director, and the captain thought it of sufficient importance to bring the Marconigram to you. You of course appreciated that it meant you were approaching ice ?" – "Yes."

"And would be passing through the region indicated in that message ?" – "I could not tell about that. I presumed so."

"And therefore it behoved those responsible for the navigation of the ship to be very careful?" – "Naturally ..."

Lord Mersey: "Is your position that in clear weather, day or night, there need be no reduction of speed although the officer knows he is in the ice region ?" – "That is right; if he can see far enough to clear the ice."

Evidence at the "Titanic" Inquiry, Westminster

Archie Jewell, twenty-three years of age, said he was one of the six look-out men of the *Titanic.* On the Sunday night the casualty occurred he was in the crow's nest from eight to ten o'clock with his fellow look-out, who was also saved.

The Solicitor-General: "Were there any look-out men on duty on any other part of the ship ?"

"No, so long as the weather is clear, and it was clear that night."

"Do you remember any message coming to you about ice?" – "Yes, sir, about 9.30 by telephone from the officer on the bridge."

"What was the message ?" – "To keep a look-out for all ice, big and small."

"Did you see any ice?" – "No; I passed word along to the man, relieving me at ten o'clock.

Joseph Scarrott, an A.B. on board the *Titanic,* said that on the Sunday night she was wrecked his watch was from eight to twelve o'clock. His duty was to stand by on call in case he might be wanted for anything whatever.

It was about half-past eleven o'clock when he heard three bells from the crow's nest. About eight minutes afterwards there was an impact followed by a vibration as if the engines were turned full speed astern.

J. Bernard Walker, writing in *The Scientific American* of New York, points out that the *Great Eastern* had a double shell extending well above the water-line and that subsequently this excellent protection was wholly omitted and that it was not until hard facts proved the egg-shell nature of the succeeding ships that the double bottom was reintroduced.

"Although the minute subdivision of the interior of a warship cannot be adopted on an ocean liner," he continues, "without seriously interfering with the placing and operation of the large boiler and engine equipment it is possible to introduce the longitudinal torpedo bulkhead of the warship and utilise the space between this bulkhead and the side of the ship for coal bunkers. The protective arrangement was one of the structural elements which the British Admiralty insisted upon in the case of the *Lusitania* and *Mauretania,* when in consideration of their receiving a heavy Government subsidy the company agreed to build them with certain safety provisions which would render them available as auxiliary cruisers should they be required by the British Government in time of war.

There is a continuous line of bulkheads on each side of the engine and boiler rooms extending from the after-transverse bulkhead of the engine-room to the forward-transverse bulkhead of the boiler-rooms. In the wake of the boiler-rooms the space thus formed is utilised for coal bunkers. Now it will be evident that if the *Mauretania* had struck the long glancing blow which sank the *Titanic* and had fractured the plating or started the seams throughout the length of several compartments the inflow of water would have been restrained by the coal bunkers, and since they would have been at least partially filled with rather finely-subdivided coal the weight of water taken into the ship would have been relatively insignificant compared with that which had access to the whole width of the *Titanic* in such compartments as were leaking.

"Referring to the *Titanic,* the coal bunkers were arranged transversly of the ship and against the main transverse bulkhead. This

The *Titanic* sails on her only voyage (1912). The story of how the *Titanic* went down on her inaugural voyage has never been paralleled. Icebergs were among the most dreaded dangers to navigation and the *Titanic* was struck a glancing blow that ripped open her starboard side. The disaster illuminated the need for reform and led directly to the foundation of the International Ice Patrol in 1914. Photograph by W.J. Day.

permitted the boilers to be placed abreast in lines extending entirely across the ship. For convenience in firing this was an admirable arrangement, bringing the coal supply immediately in front of the fire doors. From the viewpoint of safety, however, it proved to be fatal, for it is evident that any rupture of the outside skin of the ship admitted water to the whole of the compartment affected.

"It will be evident, even to the layman, that as between the longitudinal bunkers of the *Mauretania* and the transverse bunkers of the *Titanic* the system adopted on the former ship is immeasurably superior."

IMPROVEMENTS SUGGESTED BY TITANIC DISASTER
The Sphere, 1912

Improvements in life-saving devices will probably be fitted in the liners of the immediate future as a result of the *Titanic* disaster. The strengthening of the bows, the better subdivision by transverse bulkheads and the addition of a longitudinal bulkhead will be improvements in the right direction. The wireless cabin would have an independent power station on the upper deck, whilst another power station for generating electrical

55

The *Ocean Post*,
journal of the
Holland-America
Line, one of the main
steamship companies
linking Europe with
New York. There was
a printing shop
aboard ship,
responsible for
printing menu cards,
programmes, and the
ship's newspaper.
This was usually a
daily publication with
news received by
wireless telegraphy.
Ashore, reports of
arrivals and
departures were
regular newspaper
features.

power could be situated further aft, and, in case of accident to either of the masts which would bring down the wireless aerials, reserve wires would be placed between the high funnels, and two or three operators would be carried and an alarm bell fitted. The boats would be motor-driven and a life raft would find a place on the poop. Protection to the forward plates would be added. Though at present impracticable, it has been suggested that one solution would be to have electrical devices fitted amidships to weaken the structure of the hull between the two great weights, so that in case of accident the hull could thus be weakened and the weight of the machinery and water in the liner would practically tear the vessel in twain, the flooded half sinking, leaving the undamaged portion afloat.

SHIP AND SHORE COMMUNICATION
L. H. Thomas

Ship-and-shore communication is divided up between several bands of wavelengths. Before 1919 nearly all ships were equipped with spark apparatus, the only merits of which were cheapness and simplicity. The average spark signal was broadly tuned and caused serious interference, at close quarters, over a wide band of wavelengths. Since 1927, when the International Radiotelegraph Conference was held in Washington, all transmitters with a rating in excess of 300 watts have been of the valve type. Receiving apparatus of the valve type, however, was used for some time before 1927, on account of the obvious limitations of the crystal and earlier types of receiver.

The standard valve receiver supplied to shipping by the Marconi Company was built in three units comprising, a receiver tuning from 180 to 3,000 metres, a long-wave panel tuning from 3,000 to 20,000 metres, and an amplifier. The same company's more modern equipment covers all wavelengths from 15 to 20,000 metres.

Most of the safety services are handled, nowadays, on the 600-to 800-metre wave-band. Efforts have been made to clear this band of ordinary traffic so as to free it from interference and to render it more reliable for the vitally important safety service. Since the development of short-wave working, a great amount of the long-distance communication between ships and shore is carried out on wavelengths below 60 metres.

The most frequent type of message passing between ships and shore is the ordinary radio-telegram. This may be coded or sent in plain language, and is transmitted and delivered in the same way as an ordinary telegram. About 60 per cent of the messages transmitted relate to the ship's business, such as arrangements to be made before entering ports, alterations in routes and the ordering of food and equipment.

Passengers' business affairs are also largely concerned, and the remainder of the traffic consists of trivial social messages. In the course of handling routine traffic, shore stations receive a large amount of information concerning the position and movements of ships. Such information is forwarded to Lloyd's by the coastal stations.

Long-Distance Telephone
Such stations are so arranged that their reliable ranges overlap considerably. A small ship proceeding coastwise may thus remain continuously in touch with her owners or with a point on shore. A larger ship, with more powerful equipment, may establish

Far left. Palm Court and stairs. During the early years of the century decoration was intended to overwhelm. Passengers could join in the gaiety of the Palm Court, Winter Garden or Verandah café.

Left. Post-war modern. View of the first class saloon of the *Orcades,* launched in 1947 for the Orient Line.

this class of work is carried out entirely on the short waves. Owners of ordinary short-wave receivers may intercept conversations between British telephone subscribers and their friends on board the *Queen Mary, Empress of Britain, Bremen, Europa, Normandie* and a few other large liners which have telephony installations.

THE OCEAN LINER
The Architects' Journal, 1922

In his own province the naval architect is superb, unapproachable, is in his own way a great artist as well as a great engineer, and he is amazingly efficient – his is a constant warfare against natural forces, and nature does not condone mistakes, particularly mistakes upon the sea.

His creations are surprisingly beautiful – the least imaginative of us have stood spellbound by the sheer beauty of line and form of these great birds of passage.

The beauty is in a large measure unconscious and is the result of an exact use of material and of a scientific application of ends to means.

It is when he leaves his own sphere and descends into the regions of the less happily circumstanced land architect that he is not

Left. Window display for the Austin Reed concession aboard the *Queen Mary.* Galleries were employed as writing rooms or small saloons and led to the main entrance where shops were established.

communication with her destination before her voyage has begun. Ships on the North Atlantic route can communicate with Canada and with the United States while they are still in Southampton Water, and their transmissions are frequently heard in Great Britain while the ships are in sight of the American coast.

Ship-to-shore telephony is a service provided almost entirely for the convenience of passengers, and only a handful of the largest liners are equipped for this work. Their traffic is handled by the G.P.O. station at Rugby, and

quite so successful. Or rather when he hands over that portion of his ship to the mere decorator, for it is well nigh impossible to believe that any man who can lay down the lines of a great ship could condescend to the trivialities and vulgarities that mar the public rooms of so many of our great liners.

One magnificent ship visited was ruined by the low note of its decoration. The dining-room with its carved and twisted mahogany of tortuous shapes, highly polished and inlaid with masses of mother-of-pearl, its windows of the crudest stained glass, suggested nothing so much as a glorified gin palace. The lounge or drawing-room was not much better: instead of mahogany there was oak carved with nasty little squiggles which vainly imagined themselves to be indicative of Louis XV, and furniture that would have disgraced the worst type of suburban lodging house.

By contrast there are ships such as the *Aquitania,* the *Berengaria,* and the *Majestic,* where the planning and the decoration of the passengers' accommodation reach a very high standard; one need scarcely add that in each case a land architect collaborated with the naval architect to produce this happy result.

The naval architect's incessant demand is for reduced weight (particularly on the upper decks), and for economy of space, and this in itself would appear to suggest a scheme of treatment widely different from the stone proportions of our land buildings. The public rooms of any one class equal, in size and complexity of design, a large public building! Many of the private suites of rooms on the larger ships are of the extent of a small house or flat, whilst in addition there are hundreds of cabins forming long streets, all demanding consideration and treatment at the hand of the architect.

There is an unlimited scope for the land architect in connection with big ships; and when it is remembered that the life of these ships is only some twenty or twenty-five years, so that new ships are constantly being built, the importance of the subject becomes very apparent. The passenger accommodation should be planned to permit easy and quick egress in case of fire, and, at the same time, direct approach for fighting the fire. It should be so arranged that an outbreak may be restricted as far as possible to a definite section.

Fire at sea is the sailor's nightmare, and should an outbreak occur it is very difficult to keep it localised. Consequently, large sections of the ship may be gutted before the fire is brought under-control.

It is open to question whether long and narrow passages filled with smoke are convenient for the passenger escaping from the fire or for the fireman fighting it.

Another point for the untutored is the question of vibration and the possibility of consequent rattle.

All parts of the structure, fittings, details, etc., in the sleeping cabins, state rooms and public rooms should be so designed and fitted that the vibration of the ship does not cause them to rattle; also it is desirable to avoid using flexible surfaces likely to vibrate and produce a drumming sound. Everything must be well and firmly fixed. All parts of the accommodation should be planned as far as possible to allow easy ventilation with fresh warm air and without draught.

Coming to the question of water supply, only the most important suites and cabins have water laid on, in the others small receptacles have to be filled every day. There does not appear to be any good reason why fresh water should not be laid on to every sleeping cabin and state-room, provided it is borne in mind that fresh water on board ship is somewhat costly, inasmuch as it is produced almost entirely by distillation, and, as every sailor knows, the conservation of the water supply is of primary importance. Warm water is also costly, as steam must be expended in heating it – but it might be possible, under some carefully contrived system of rationing, to lay on both hot and cold water to all cabins and so save an infinite amount of labour.

It is very difficult to keep a ship absolutely free from vermin such as rats, cockroaches, and other pests; on some routes in certain parts of the world it is absolutely impossible to do so. In considering the suitability of materials for

decoration and design of the passenger accommodation, it is necessary to remember that a ship in her many journeys over the world may experience all extremes of atmospheric temperature and humidity. As far as the exterior of the ship goes, the land architect gets very little opportunity. The one last piece of decoration left him is the ornamental work on the counter at the stern – even this is rigorously cut out on some modern ships. When it is well-designed, as, for instance, on the *Berengaria,* it gives an additional touch of tradition that adds to the interest and beauty of the ship. It is the last relic of the great and glorious poops of the old sailing ships that is left to us. Naval architects call this work "gilt ginger-bread".

MODERN OCEAN RAIDERS
Lt.-Com. E. Keble Chatterton

In the olden days of sail, so long as a ship had fresh water, salt beef and biscuits, she was independent of the shore and could roam the seas for three or four years, varied by an occasional stoppage at the back of some lonely island or secluded bay, where her foul hull could be cleaned after careening. But a modern steamship is far less independent, and is entirely at the mercy of her fuel.

Moreover, there comes a time when boilers must be cleaned and engines overhauled, necessitating repairs that demand the facilities of a dockyard. If, too, she is a fast steamer, then every few days she must replenish fuel, and this means that colliers must meet her on a given date at a particular rendezvous. How, amid the risks of war and the uncertainties of events, can this be guaranteed ? If the raider is running short of fuel, how can she avoid being herself captured when some smart grey naval unit comes rushing towards her?

It was the *Emden* which sought to overcome this difficulty by capturing every collier she met, putting a prize crew on board, and ordering the colliers to wait in some assigned locality. Other raiders copied that idea with considerable success, and even robbed vessels carrying general cargo; but the game could not

be easy, and was influenced by geographical conditions. To empty a steamer alongside her in the open sea and damage both hulls, as the ocean swell rendered fend-offs useless, was to ruin both vessels – though this method had to be attempted more than once. Generally speaking, although transference could be made if fairly conveniently close to some island of the Indian Ocean, it was barely practicable in the wide Atlantic.

Secret Rendezvous
The Germans, however, fared well, largely because of their forethought. Six years before the war they had issued instructions to their liner captains as to what would be their duties should hostilities break out; a "Cruiser Handbook" had been compiled, giving a list of secret rendezvous whither liners could make and be fitted with guns. One such spot was near the Bahamas and another was off the lonely South Atlantic island of Trinidad, east of Brazil. It was here that the *Cap Trafalgar*

"Convoy", by John Everett. The artist Norman Wilkinson had proposed the idea of dazzle camouflage in 1917. Painting vessels with contrasting patches confused the enemy (especially submarines) as to a vessel's size, type and direction. The designs were much influenced by Cubist, or Vorticist, painting.

The luxurious first class saloon of the *Homeric*, 1922. Constructed at the Schichau shipyards in Danzig, Germany for Norddeutscher Lloyd in 1913, the *Homeric* was eventually surrendered and taken over by White Star following the Armistice.

"On Board the *Columbia*", by Phil May, most economical of draughtsmen and well-known *Punch* artist. The caption reads "Westward Ho! On Board A German Liner Bound For New York". A midday concert on deck was the customary offering from the ship's orchestra.

bunkered during the first weeks of the war, and here that the Hamburg-Amerika *Navarra,* with supplies for German cruisers, was found on November 11, 1914, by the British armed merchant cruiser *Orama.* After a chase, the *Orama* sank the *Navarra* but rescued the crew. Another feature of the Germans' foresight was the arrangement of supply centres, each supervised by a supply officer north, east, west and south of the Atlantic trade area. The principal centres were at New York, Las Palmas, Havana, Rio de Janeiro and Buenos Aires, and smaller centres were located at the Danish (now American) island of St. Thomas in the West Indies, at Para, Pernambuco, Bahia, and Santos in Brazil, at Montevideo in Uruguay, and at Punta Arenas in the Magellan Straits.

By means of wireless and telegraph cables this remarkable chain maintained an unbroken connection with Berlin through New York. Even such spots as Lome, in Togoland, Tenerife, in the Canaries, and Horta, in the Azores, were not too remote for the organization. Each supply officer had to ensure that the requisite number of colliers could be found in his area, so that any raider had only to look into the "Cruiser Handbook", select her rendezvous, arrive, and go alongside for bunkering without unnecessary wirelessing.

GERMAN SHIPPING
Frank C. Bowen

The German mercantile marine is remarkable not only for its success under an extreme measure of State control, but also for the manner in which it has revived since the war of 1914-18. Before the war the German tonnage was 11.1 per cent of the world's total. After the war it dropped almost to nothing, due to the enforcement of the surrender of merchant ships in reparation for the campaign of submarine warfare.

In 1936 German shipping climbed back to 5.8 per cent of a much larger total in the world. When so many ships are still laid up, it is even more remarkable that the German mercantile marine can claim to be one of the most up-to-date services in the globe. This

THE BAND.

"Even this morning when most of us are sufficiently recovered to be critical, its brazen sound is grateful it makes us think less of the Fatherland we have left than of the land we're going to."

WESTWARD HO! ON BOARD A GERMAN LINER BOUND F

a bird of ill omen.

Russian Journalism.

a Tyrolean.

EW YORK

achievement has been due largely to Government measures. Under the Treaty of Versailles, Germany had to cede to the Allies all her merchant ships of 1,600 tons gross or over, half of those between 1,000 and 1,600 tons, and a quarter of the fishing fleet. She also agreed to build for the Allied and Associated Government a maximum of 200,000 tons gross of shipping annually for three years; but this provision was waived by common consent and "reparations in kind" were substituted.

The Allied shipowners who had taken over the German ships soon found that they had a surplus, and the slump was inevitable. Many of the more useful vessels found their way back to the German flag, but the authorities were careful that these ships, quite old by this time, were admitted only to relieve immediate necessities and not to interfere with the new building programme.

The programme had been carefully thought out during the war and a scheme of Government loans drawn up. In the emergency it was necessary to modify this scheme, and little could be done before 1921; but it formed a basis and owners and builders co-operated excellently. Different yards specialized in building different types of

The *Amerika* of 1903. With designs by the celebrated designer, Charles Mewès, and catering overseen by the famous hotelier, César Ritz, this German liner was among the smartest. Several international restaurateurs operated successful concessions afloat during the Golden Years.

vessels. The naval dockyards which had been suppressed under the Treaty of Versailles were put to commercial use and the inefficient and old-fashioned shipbuilding yards were drastically rationalized.

German inventors also put in an immense amount of useful effort in improving the economy of their ships in the fuel consumption of the machinery and in the improvement of hull forms. These improvements in the design of the hull reduced the resistance of the ship in the water and permitted the same results to be attained with a much smaller horse-power.

The much-discussed rotor ship, the Oertz streamline rudder, the improved streamlining of funnels and superstructure, the bulbous bow and the Maier hull form, all secured the results aimed at and brought valuable business to the country, in addition to making Germany's own ships more efficient.

Among the engine-room improvements was the Lentz engine, which increased the thermodynamic efficiency of the steam reciprocating engine. The Lentz engine, however, has been applied only to a small number of ships as compared with the Bauer Wach turbine.

The Bauer Wach exhaust turbine overcame the difficulty of unequal torque and permitted a low-pressure turbine to get the last ounce of power out of the steam from the last low-pressure stage before it entered the condensers. Many improvements were also introduced into German diesel engines, adding to their economy, reducing their cost and weight, and making them so much more compact that they interfered even less with the carrying capacity of the ship.

The single-ship company, which is such a feature of British and Scandinavian shipping, was almost unknown; but from 1925 onwards this policy was carried to far greater lengths and nearly all the companies of any importance were gathered into a few big groups headed by the Hamburg-Amerika line and Norddeutscher Lloyd (North German Lloyd).

It appeared at first that this would inevitably lead to greater economy, but in practice the Germans were to learn what the British had

Doppelschrauben-Postdampfer „Amerika"

learned before, that a shipping concern can become too big and cumbersome, and that efficiency is liable to be lost when services of an entirely different nature are gathered together. That realization, however, was to come later. When it did, the authorities were not afraid to admit their mistake and to begin a policy of decentralization which was just as energetic as the previous grouping movement.

At the same time unnecessary cut-throat competition within Germany was abolished, and even the old rivalry between the Hamburg-Amerika and North German Lloyd companies, inherited from the bitter feuds and quarrels of Bremen and Hamburg within the Hanseatic League in the old days, had to give way to a reasonable working agreement between the companies.

The North German Lloyd, repeating its daring experiment with the *Kaiser Wilhelm der Grosse* in 1897, put the merchant service in the forefront of popular interest by building the *Bremen* and the *Europa*. These ships won back the Blue Riband of the Atlantic that had been held by the Cunard liner *Mauretania* for the record period of twenty years.

This remarkable achievement did all that was expected. It took place in the middle of the worst slump in history, but it brought the best of the Atlantic business to the German flag, and the North German Lloyd felt the pinch less than any other company. In one year the average passenger list of the *Europa* numbered about 500 – roughly fifty per cent more than that of any other liner crossing the Atlantic. The slump, however, had a marked effect on the prosperity of German shipping in general. Although heavy losses were sustained by individual shareholders and workers, the owners co-operated with the Government in reducing the effects as much as possible. A voyage bonus was paid, the State shouldered a good many of the heavy charges for social service which were a great handicap to German industry of all kinds, and it also seized the opportunity of clearing the lists of the less efficient tonnage.

Large numbers of the surrendered ships, built before the war and bought back from the Allies, were ruthlessly scrapped. When the Government encouraged the building of new and up-to-date tonnage it gave its help on condition that two tons of old shipping should be broken up for every new ton built. The decentralization policy, and the partial breaking up of the big groups into their most efficient constituents took place at the same time. When the Nazi regime came into power it carried on the shipping policy of its predecessors with even greater vigour, although the benefits that it granted were nearly all accompanied by conditions which many considered to be harsh.

So the German merchant service today is a remarkably efficient organization. There are few ships laid up for lack of employment, although, as in every other country, they have to accept terms which leave little balance after the expenses have been paid, even with the financial assistance that is allowed by the Government.

After the Great War, at the first opportunity, German services were again pushing out on the old routes, modestly and often in partnership with companies under Allied flags, but gradually with more self-assurance and definite purpose. The ships were generally of moderate size but of good speed and the services were excellently organized so that they soon returned to their old favour. Alliances are now seldom found and in many conferences it is the German companies which have the premier position.

Apart from the Atlantic routes, the North German Lloyd maintains services to the Straits

Hamburg-Amerika Line, aka Hapag, started in 1847. Hapag's Chairman, Albert Ballin, built large express steamers for the transatlantic passenger traffic and was the first shipowner to commission specialist interior decorators and *chef-de-cuisine*. By 1914, Hapag had displaced all rivals to become the world's largest shipping concern and Germany's foremost Atlantic passenger carrier.

Settlements and the Far East, North Pacific, Central America and the West Indies, Brazil, the west coast of South America and Australia. The Far Eastern passenger service, maintained by the liners *Scharnhorst, Gneisenau* and *Potsdam,* is particularly striking. Liners of more than 18,000 tons gross, the *Scharnhorst* and her two sisters were built in 1935 for this service.

The Hamburg-Amerika company is more restricted in its activities than its Bremen rivals but it maintains a large number of services, some of them in partnership with other German lines and mostly to various parts of the Western Hemisphere.

The Woermann, Deutsche Ost-Afrika and Hamburg-Bremen-Afrika Lines are all interested in the African services. The Horn Line is mainly concerned with the West Indies and Central America, the Hansard Line with the Indian Ocean and the Hamburg South American Line with several services to the Latin-American republics.

North Atlantic Services

Before the war of 1914-18 the German lines carried an enormous number of emigrants to the United States, not only from Germany itself but from all the countries of Eastern Europe. The control and final disappearance of the emigrant business was a serious loss to the German companies, but they made it up to a great extent by developing the tourist business.

As figureheads of the Western Ocean fleet the North German Lloyd's *Bremen* and *Europa* stand by themselves, for most of the other German ships running across the Atlantic are of comparatively moderate size and speed. The majority of them are steam-driven, but geared diesels have been tried with success.

HOUSE FLAGS AND FUNNELS
Boyd Cable

In the early days of steamers, burning any kind of coal with imperfect combustion, it was natural that funnels should nearly all be painted black to avoid showing the smoke grime. But owners then had no tradition or rule of funnel colours or markings and kept no record of them. The only clues to them now are in old paintings and prints. These, in fact, show how irregular or erratic a line's funnel colours were.

The P. & O., for example, did not always have the black hulls and funnels and buff upperworks now so widely known over the whole of the Eastern hemisphere. Some of its first little paddle steamers had white or red funnels with black tops; and before the Suez Canal opened, the ships from Egypt to India had white hulls.

STRATHNAVER

TE · SISTERS

The Blue Funnel Line

BLAND LINE
S.S. GIBEL SARSAR

Above. The Blue Funnel Line, starting from Liverpool, ran a monthly service, via the Suez Canal and Shanghai, to Yokohoma in Japan. They were also one of the prominent British companies trading with South America.

Below. Other latitudes: the steamship *Gibel Sarsar* of the Bland Line, who operated a Gibraltar-Tangier-Casablanca service. Europa Point, at the south end of Gibraltar, is 14 miles from the African coast.

There was therefore an old precedent for the colouring of the *Strathmore* and two other "Straths" of the P. & O. These luxury liners are known as "the White Sisters", because both ships are painted in gleaming white from the red "boot-topping" along the waterline to the golden-yellow funnel's foot.

There is, however, one line that takes its name from its ships' funnels, and there is a well authenticated tale of how the funnel colour was first adopted.

The owner of the first steamer bought by Holt's had just died. In accordance with ancient sea custom (still followed in rare instances) a blue band had to be painted round the hull as a sign of mourning.

The ship, bought as she lay, had on board numerous drums of blue paint. The paint was used up on the funnel, and the same distinctive shade of blue has ever since marked the vessels of the Blue Funnel Line.

Bibby Bros., one of our oldest shipping firms, founded in 1807, and the Leyland Line have funnels of an unusual "salmon pink"; and both, curiously, had for many years the same plain red flag. The Bibby family crest on one, and a cross through the other, now distinguish them. There are many more flags of historic origin and meaning, as in Shaw, Savill & Albion's adaptation of the first Maori national flag, and the Anchor Line's four links of cable representing the four founder brothers.

As the flags were worn by sail and steam, by vessels with single, compound, triple expansion, turbine, oil-fired and internal combustion engines, so they are now being worn by their shipowner company's aircraft. The General Steam Navigation Co., founded with paddle-steamers in 1824, started in 1935 to issue tickets that took passengers from London to Ramsgate by aeroplane, thence to return by pleasure steamers. The aeroplanes displayed the flag of the company. In this way the routine of the newest form of transport preserved the traditions of one of the oldest.

Some Atlantic liners carry aircraft to speed up the last lap of the passage for mail or passengers. And in January, 1936, the Union Steam Ship Company of New Zealand opened a daily air service between North Island and South Island. In this practical and prosaic age, it is good that we can still preserve a measure of sentiment; and in few ways can we better preserve, treasure and perpetuate our maritime sentiment, history and tradition than in the house flag symbols of the Merchant Navy.

Funnel of the *Queen Mary* by Madame Yevonde, the English society photographer commissioned by America's
Fortune Magazine to cover the fitting-out of the Cunard liner in John Brown's shipyard in 1936.
Despite Cunard's reluctance to co-operate and difficulties hauling Yevonde's equipment aboard,
Fortune were delighted with the results of the commission.

IN QUICK TIME

"we are such stuff as
dreams are made on"

"The Tempest" William Shakespeare

THE BLUE RIBAND OF THE ATLANTIC
Frank C. Bowen

Sailing-ship races with China tea, and, to a lesser extent, with Australian wool, attracted almost as much attention in the middle of the nineteenth century as the Derby does to-day. The names of ships and of their captains were household words then, even with the lay public. Nowadays there is keen interest in the Blue Riband of the Atlantic, which is the subject of continual speculation. There is ample justification for this interest. Not only is the story of the record, and of the struggle for its possession, a fascinating one, but also on the practical side the competition has exercised great influence on the technical improvement of the steamer.

In the early days there was little effort to attain speed on the Western Ocean, the only fast Atlantic ships being the slavers, which did not carry voluntary passengers *(sic,* ed.). Transatlantic trade began on a big scale after Waterloo. Sailing packets were fine ships and developed rapidly when, after a lapse of time, owners made a real attempt to improve their speed; but the owners took few pains to make their performances known. Steam came in gradually, and the heavy coal consumption of the primitive boilers prevented any great effort to accelerate the service.

Brunel's steamer, the *Great Western,* might be described as the first holder of the Atlantic record, for she undoubtedly beat her rival, the *Sirius,* to New York in 1838. But the race was more or less accidental, for the steamers started from different points. That they finished at New York on the same day, with the *Great Western's* passage from Bristol five days shorter than that of the *Sirius* from Cork, surprised all concerned. The winner's average was 8.2 knots, a figure that gives a starting line to the competition.

In 1840 the Cunard Company began operations with four sister ships. It was that feature which made their success; individually many of their competitors' steamers were far better, but they were a mixed collection.

Neither the Cunard nor any other owner said much about speed, although the average of the Cunarders was much better than that of the sailing packets. On her maiden passage the pioneer *Britannia* averaged 8.5 knots between Liverpool and Halifax; but that was scarcely a fair test, because there were doubts about her coal consumption, and her people were naturally anxious to eke out their supplies. Later in the same year she did the eastward run from Halifax to Liverpool at an average of 10.56 knots. The *Acadia,* the best steamer of the original quartet, logged records of 9.25 knots westward and 10.75 eastward, later improving on the eastward performance by a fraction of a knot. The design of the pioneer class was only slightly improved in the *Hibernia* type; but the *Hibernia* herself averaged 11.67 knots eastward and the *Asia,* a rather bigger ship built in 1850, contrived 12.12 knots westbound, and slightly lowered the eastward record.

In the 'forties of the last century the Americans were enjoying a high reputation for the speed of their sailing ships. When they were in such keen competition with the Cunard Company for the Atlantic business they naturally wanted to make the most of this, and built their packet ships for speed. They were remarkable vessels, but they could not equal the steamers in either sustained speed or general average of passage. In 1847 the Americans made their first serious attempt in transatlantic steam navigation with the subsidized Ocean Steam Navigation Co.'s service. It was a daring move, for American shipbuilders and engineers had no experience of building such ships or their machinery. Thus it is not surprising that their design was faulty, their boilers too small to keep the engines in steam, and their paddles too deeply submerged. The result was that they failed to beat the Cunarders' time, and eleven-day passages were their best.

Although the Ocean Company's steamers were a failure, the Americans were determined to have their share of the trade, and the Collins Line was begun with Government help. Collins himself had long experience with transatlantic sailing ships and built, in 1849,

68

A.M. Cassandre's lithograph for *L'Atlantique* (1931). One of the finest commercial artists of his day, Cassandre here draws the viewer's eye upwards. The diminutive tug-boat further emphasises the enormous scale of the ship. Competition was stiff on the South Atlantic route from Europe. In times of prosperity South Americans were frequent travellers to the Continent, demanding luxury on a lavish scale.

the wooden paddle-steamers *Arctic, Baltic, Atlantic* and *Pacific* – ships whose tonnage of nearly 3,000 made them considerably bigger than the contemporary Cunarders. They were undoubtedly the most luxuriously fitted ships of their day, although with their straight stems and high sides they seemed ugly to those accustomed to graceful clipper bows. They cost much more to build than the estimate and the company had to call on the United States Treasury for further assistance; but they got the cream of the traffic. As new ships, the *Baltic* broke the westward record with an average of 13 knots, and the *Pacific* maintained the same speed to the eastward, although they had to burn nearly 100 tons of coal a day to do so, and their bunkers occupied a large part of their hulls. In 1852 the *Arctic* lowered the *Pacific's* eastward time with 13.25 knots. The Cunarders had to take second place until a sudden reversal of American political feeling towards the subsidy caused the complete ruin of the Collins Line and the withdrawal of its service. Meanwhile, a new rival had appeared, although it was not initially recognized as such; in 1850 William Inman started his steamship company. While the Cunard Company was building big paddlers he went in for smaller, but more efficient, iron screw steamers, which were sufficiently economical in fuel and space to permit him to carry emigrants. At first he was content to do this with tonnage of moderate speed.

The Cunard directors, determined that the company should regain its former position, built some remarkably fine paddle-steamers. The *Arabia,* the last wooden ship in the fleet, was a fast vessel in smooth water, but a failure on the Atlantic. Her speed dropped rapidly in rough water, her powerful engines shook her hull to pieces, and her boilers consumed 120 tons of coal a day. In the *Persia,* perhaps the most beautiful of paddle-liners, they turned to an iron hull. In 1856 she beat the eastward record with an average of 13.75 knots, although the *Baltic's* westward record of 13 knots stood until the *Scotia* lowered it to 13.6 knots in 1864, having previously beaten the *Persia* on the eastward run with 14 knots.

These fine ships were built largely because of danger which threatened from another quarter. In the 'fifties Irish political influence was great, and the scheme to establish a service from Galway in Western Ireland to St. John's, Newfoundland, and New York received such strong political backing that the Post Office gave the promoters a mail subsidy against the Cunard. Had they been able to do what they promised it would certainly have been a good bargain. Basing their estimates on the achievements of the cross-Channel packets, the promoters undertook to run to St. John's in six days and to New York in seven. To the former port they would carry telegraphic messages to be sent over the land wires, as the Atlantic cable was not yet working.

For this service they ordered four paddle-steamers of about 3,000 tons at a cost of about £95,000 each. It was estimated that their powerful engines would drive them at 17.5 knots in smooth water if they were given the lightest possible hulls. Disaster came as soon as they ventured into water which was not smooth. The *Connaught* was burned out when she was on the point of foundering in the Atlantic, the *Columbia* took seventeen days on her maiden voyage instead of the contract seven days, and arrived leaking so badly that she had to be reconstructed, and the *Hibernia* had to be rebuilt before she could start out at all. The unfortunate company collapsed.

Then the competition of the Inman Line began to develop. William Inman had been steadily improving his steamers and appreciated the publicity value of the Blue Riband just as much as Collins had done. His first success was in 1867 with the *City of Paris,* making the shortest westerly passage, which was given great publicity in Europe and the United States, although it was really due entirely to the short route selected; the average speed was slightly less than that of *Scotia.* But in 1869 the *City of Brussels* undoubtedly beat the *Scotia's* best eastward time by half a knot, averaging 14.5 knots. There was great rivalry between the Cunard and the Inman Lines in the 'sixties, and the latter's screw ships certainly had the advantage over the Cunard's paddlers.

In 1867 the Cunard screw vessel, *Russia,* secured the eastward record with an average of 14.22 knots, but within a month she had lost it to the *City of Brussels* with 14.66 knots. In 1870 another competitor appeared in the White Star Line. Its Atlantic liners were built on an entirely new principle, on which Edward Harland, of Harland and Wolff, the Belfast shipbuilders, staked everything and made his reputation. These ships were very long, arranged internally on a novel principle and, with their single funnel and four masts, introduced a new rig. In 1872 the *Adriatic* beat the westward record with an average of 14.5 knots, and in the following year *Baltic* took the eastward average up to 15 knots. The rivalry thus changed to one between the Inman and White Star Companies, the Cunard letting the record go and building inferior ships for a time. This caused a bitter newspaper controversy. Both companies built new tonnage, of which the White Star *Germanic* and *Britannic* were the most conspicuous ships. Eastward, the *City of Berlin* averaged 15.25 knots in 1875, the *Germanic* contriving 15.75 knots in the following year, only to lose the record to her sister the *Britannic* with 16 knots in the same year. Westward, the *City of Berlin's* 15 knots logged in 1865 was beaten by the *Britannic's* 15.25 in 1876 and by the *Germanic's* 15.5 in 1877. In the same year the *Britannic* beat her sister on time alone, not in average speed.

Noticing the success of the Inman Company in breaking into the saloon business, the Guion Line, which also had originally carried on a purely emigrant business, made its first attempt to build record-breakers in 1872 with the freak steamers *Montana* and *Dakota.* They were, perhaps, the most curious ships put on the Atlantic, both in hull and in machinery. The machinery included water-tube boilers – the first to be tried in big ships – working at 100 lb. pressure. The engineers hoped that these ships would contrive 17 knots with remarkable economy, but they were disappointed.

The *Montana* disabled all ten of her water-tube boilers on her passage from the builders and was refused a passenger licence until they had been replaced with something safer. Both engines and boilers were constantly breaking down and neither ship could approach 17 knots, although the coal consumption was colossal. The *Dakota* was wrecked in 1877 and the *Montana* in 1880, and the company was well rid of them.

Despite their failure, S. B. Guion, who controlled the company, persisted in his ambition, but wisely went to one of the best shipbuilders in the country, John Elder & Co., who later became the Fairfield Yard. In 1879 they built him the *Arizona* the first ship to be nicknamed the "Atlantic Greyhound" and the first to be propelled by a three-crank compound engine. Her design was daring, but Sir William Pearce, the head of Fairfield's, had faith in himself which was amply justified. In 1879 the *Arizona* secured the eastward record with a fraction of a knot more than the *Britannic's* average, and in the following year she equalled her speed westward, securing a slightly better time by the shorter route. The general principles of her design were followed with slight improvements in the *Alaska,* which quickly proved itself by securing both records in 1882, averaging 16.75 knots eastward and 16 westward.

Made bold by the publicity which the Guion steamers' records had obtained, a third emigrant company, the National Line, determined to try the same policy and built the *America,* a particularly beautiful clipper-stemmed ship, which brought the eastward average up to 17.5 knots. But with this record her luck ended. The saloon business could not support so many crack ships as had been put on service, and the National Line made the mistake of attempting to run its first-class service with the *America* only. No unbalanced service has yet succeeded on the Western Ocean and, losing large sums on her operation, the line eventually sold her to Italy for conversion into a cruiser. Meanwhile, the third Guion liner, the famous *Oregon,* had been delivered, a further improvement on the *Alaska.* In 1884 she secured both records, the eastward with an average of 18.5 knots and the westward with 19. But the company's receipts were not sufficient to pay the instalments due

71

Clydebank shipbuilders J&G Thomson were originally noted for speed. The Inman Line went to them for the *City of New York* (seen here in a painting by the Spanish artist, Raphael Monleon y Torres). She was the first transatlantic express to exceed 10,000 tons, and, coupled with the *City of Paris,* she competed against White Star's *Teutonic* and *Majestic.* Their rivalry took the Atlantic speed-record to over twenty knots for the first time.

on the ships. The *Oregon,* which was widely discussed as the first ship to reach New York in less than a week, was transferred to the Cunard Line, under whose flag her career was shortened by a collision, in which she sank.

During these developments, the Inman Company had not been idle, but in 1881 took delivery of the beautiful *City of Rome,* specially designed to regain the record. Had the original design been adhered to it is probable that she would have done so, for the substitution of steel for iron in her hull had greatly reduced its weight. But supplies of shipbuilding steel were short, and in order to obtain delivery the company sanctioned the use of a large proportion of iron.

Thus her hull was much heavier than had been calculated. As she could neither make her designed speed nor carry her guaranteed cargo, she was thrown back on to the hands of her builders, who put her under the management of the Anchor Line. She was a very popular passenger ship and her speed improved later, but she was never a record breaker.

In 1884 the Cunard Company had come back into the record class with the sister ships *Umbria* and *Etruria,* going to the Fairfield Yard for them as the Guion line had done. The

transfer of the *Oregon* to the Cunard flag robbed these two ships of their principal purpose, but they were remarkably successful and popular. As with the White Star *Britannic* and *Germanic* ten years previously, they exchanged both records backwards and forwards between them by fractions of a knot; but finally the *Etruria* secured both westward and eastward records, achieving an average of 19.5 knots.

It was in the eighties that the possibilities of the Southampton record began to assume shape. Liners between the United States and the Continent had called at Southampton since the 'forties. But they were of moderate speed, and it was not until the French and German companies, Compagnie Générale Transatlantique, North German Lloyd and Hamburg-Amerika, renewed their fleets in the eighties that their speed began to approximate to that of the Liverpool ships. The Southampton record was considered as distinct from the Liverpool record on the Continent, but for the time being it did not attract any great attention in England and its publicity value was confined to the European trade. In the 'eighties, the threatened international situation provided the opportunity of

development in another direction. A number of ships were taken as auxiliary cruisers, the *Oregon* proving herself faster than any regular cruiser at manoeuvres. But they cost so much that the Admiralty determined to have a regular arrangement with the shipowners and to pay them a subsidy for crack liners which, it was then believed, would make ideal cruisers in war time.

The White Star Company first took full advantage of this subsidy arrangement, which eased the cost considerably, and it made the most of the advertisement afforded by the inspection by the German Emperor of the *Teutonic* as an auxiliary cruiser. The Inman Line immediately followed suit. The result was the construction of the White Star *Teutonic* and *Majestic,* and of the Inman *City of Paris* and *City of New York,* in 1888 and 1889. These four ships differed widely in appearance, but were evenly matched in size and speed. Rivalry between the four lasted from 1889 to 1893 and ended in the westward record being held by the *City of Paris* with an average of 21 knots, and the eastward by the *City of New York* with 20. When the Inman Line failed, the remnants of its fleet and business were taken over by the American Line, which transferred the terminus to Southampton with these two ships. They thus drew attention to the Southampton record. This had been lowered by the Hamburg-Amerika ships in the late 'eighties and early 'nineties and was held by the *Fürst Bismarck* until the Inman ships were transferred. In 1893 the Cunard Company built the *Campania* and *Lucania* at the Fairfield Yard. A fight for the record followed, ending in the *Lucania* holding both, the westward with

an average speed of 21.85 knots and the eastward with 22. Then came what was, perhaps, the most dramatic incident in the history of the Atlantic record. The North German Lloyd had been beaten by the Hamburg-Amerika and was in a serious position. After long consideration and discussion the directors decided on the daring step of risking everything in the construction of the crack ships of the Atlantic. The German Government was anxious to encourage native shipbuilding and the company took the opportunity of fixing a hard contract. Two German shipyards were to risk building two vessels of a type which they had never considered before. The trial trip was to be the maiden crossing of the Atlantic and the speed conditions were onerous. To the astonishment of the world, which had not taken German shipping and shipbuilding seriously until then, the *Kaiser Wilhelm der Grosse* came close to the Cunarder's average speed and contrived to log a time record. The *Kaiser Friedrich,* on the other hand, failed by a fraction of a knot and was thrown back on to the hands of her builders for fifteen years. It was not long before the *Kaiser Wilhelm der Grosse* won both records with an average of 22.7 knots westward and 22.8 eastward.

Meanwhile, in 1900 the Hamburg-Amerika company built the record-breaking *Deutschland,* which was a remarkably fast steamer, but did not maintain the high average, voyage after voyage, of her Bremen rival. After long consideration the directors decided to leave the record alone and to build for moderate speed with the largest size and the greatest possible measure of comfort. A similar decision had already been reached by the White Star Line which never attempted a record-breaker after 1889. The *Deutschland,* accordingly, had her power drastically reduced and became the 18-knot cruising yacht *Victoria Luise.*

But there was no doubt as to the success of the policy of the directors of the North German Lloyd. In the year after they had won the record their ships carried 25 per cent of the total number of transatlantic passengers. They improved on the *Kaiser Wilhelm der Grosse*

design with the *Kronprinz Wilhelm*, which won the westward record with 23.09 knots but the eastward on time only. The next ship was the *Kaiser Wilhelm II* which was successful on time only, and the fourth was the *Kronprincessin Cecilie,* which had no time to get into her stride before the record had passed into the hands of the Cunard Company again.

The triumph was attained by the *Lusitania* and *Mauretania*. These ships were built in 1907, with the assistance of the Government to keep the British flag in a predominant position, despite German success and the immense financial operations of the late Pierpont Morgan, who had founded the International Mercantile Marine group. The Government lent the company money on easy terms to build the two ships, which were far bigger than any previously considered. It also paid the company an annual subsidy to have them available as auxiliary cruisers, a purpose for which they proved unsuitable when war broke out. The *Lusitania* was completed first. Nursing her turbine engines, which had never before been fitted into an express steamer, she immediately won the eastward record with an average of 23.61 knots and, having found her form, the westward with 24.25. That was in 1907; two years later she brought her average westward speed up to 25.01. The *Mauretania* was a little later and took longer to get into her stride, but in 1909 she logged an eastward record at an average of 25.89 and a westward at no less than 26.06 knots. Her time from Daunt's Rock (entrance to Cork Harbour) to Sandy Hook (New York) was four days 10 hours 41 minutes, a record which stood for twenty years. With age her speed increased; while racing to the assistance of a ship in distress in appalling weather, she worked up to over 29 knots.

International Rivalry

The early days of the war proved that the express liner was useless as an auxiliary cruiser because of the difficulty in keeping her in coal, and when matters were readjusted after the Armistice there seemed to be little chance of the owners obtaining Government help on that score. It was also generally believed that the post-war traveller would demand the most reasonable fare possible, even if the ship were slower, and most companies built moderate tonnage on that assumption. But the North German Lloyd, bent on repeating the success of 1897, built the *Bremen* and the *Europa* to regain the record. Their design embodied a number of entirely novel features. They were completely successful; in 1929 the *Bremen* averaged 27.9 knots eastward and the *Europa* 27.91 knots westward.

The influx of American tourists to Europe by the northern route did not suit the Italians. With the assistance of the Government, who insisted that competition within the flag should be abolished and that the Italia Line should be formed by a combination of the rival Italian companies on the Atlantic run, they built the *Rex* and the *Conte di Savoia* the first record-breakers that they had ever considered. When the *Rex* logged the first Italian record with a westward average of 28.92 knots, with excellent air connection at Gibraltar, the service attracted many American travellers.

The diversion of the American trade to the southern route was as unpalatable to the French as the northern tendency had been to the Italians. State aid was therefore, readily given to the Compagnie Générale Transatlantique to build the great liner *Normandie.*

She gained the Blue Riband on her maiden voyage by a large margin. From Southampton to New York she made a mean speed of 29.53 knots. The highest speed recorded on this run was 31.37 knots. On the eastbound voyage her mean speed was 30.34 knots, the highest recorded speed being 30.91 knots.

Au Bord Du *Queen Mary.* **A watercolour showing deft outline drawing by Raoul Dufy on board the liner in 1936. Sea pieces were favourite subjects for the French painter and textile designer.**

SPEED AT SEA
Professor A.M. Low, 1935

Transport by water has not been speeded up in quite the spectacular fashion that transport on land and in the air have been during the last twenty years. Nevertheless, speed at sea is now considered of vital importance, and the so-called "Blue Riband of the Atlantic" – it is a real trophy presented by Mr. A. G. Hales, M.P. – is greatly coveted by maritime nations. When the *Queen Mary* undertakes her trials early next year it is expected that she will show a turn of speed that will bring this trophy proudly back to Britain.

The problems of speed at sea are fundamentally the same as those of speed on land. You have to consider friction and air resistance and, in the case of commercial transport, you have to consider the cost and the question of comfort. Owing to the length of sea voyages – even the short Atlantic crossing is, by time, a longer journey than most people under-take at a spell by train or air – comfort becomes the important factor, and designers, while sparring no effort to get those extra knots, have had to consider the possible vibration and noise. I understand that the changes that are being made in the French liner *Normandie* are designed to reduce the effect of vibration which, when going all out, has been described as terrific.

I suppose that compared with an aeroplane, the vibration and noise of the *Normandie* were not great, but the point is that it had to be endured for five days on end, whereas the

75

The *Queen Mary,*
watercolour by the
New York artist
Reginald Marsh.
Formerly an
illustrator for *Vanity
Fair, Harper's Bazaar*
and the *New York
Daily News,* Marsh
was invited to paint
murals for the
Rotunda in
the New York
Customs house in
1937. He chose as his
marine subject the
arrival of a liner into
New York harbour.

average aeroplane "hop" is only four or five hours long.

If you take the combination of comfort and speed, probably the latest ocean liners are far ahead of other forms of transport. They are slower than the slowest express train and would be left far behind by any aeroplane, but they offer the comforts of a first-class hotel The passenger can have his drinks, swim, play cricket, and even sit in his cabin and ring up almost any telephone number in the world with almost as much ease as if he were in his own house.

That has been the greatest advantage of ocean traffic over the aeroplane. Until the longest air journey is reduced to a matter of two or three days I should imagine that there will always be many people who would prefer the comfort of a liner, although when it comes to a question of pure speed, the aeroplane holds the advantage every time.

In dealing with speed at sea we have to consider friction with the air in the same way as on land. The latest liners are "streamlined". Their funnels are oval and their deck structures carefully designed to send the wind sliding past rather than pressing on it. I have heard people with some knowledge of streamlining remark that this must be mostly for show, since a simple calculation will show that air resistance has comparatively little effect on speed before speeds of fifty and sixty miles an hour are reached. This is true, but a ship often steams against a headwind which may be blowing at anything from ten to fifty miles an hour. In that event the streamlining may make a difference of five or ten miles an hour, or, putting it another way, reduce the amount of fuel used for a voyage by some hundreds of tons of coal.

Much more important at sea than the friction of the air is the friction of the water. Most of a ship's power goes to drive it through the water, and it is for this reason that the last five or six knots are often so expensive in fuel. The resistance of the water does not increase directly as the speed, but is comparable to the square of the speed. The object of the designer seeking speed or economy, or both, is,

therefore, to reduce this resistance of the water. He gives the vessel a knife-like bow and he cuts away the back. The principles are much the same as in streamlining in air, though possibly more difficult in application.

Many people may wonder why the speed of liners lags so far behind that of motor boats built for racing. Against the Atlantic liner's all-out speed of thirty knots we have Commodore Gar Wood's 124.98 m.p.h. – a gap far wider than exists between the racing and the fastest commercial aeroplanes. The difference in the sea records can be explained in the fact that the motor-boats, apart from their engines, are "stepped". They are really hydroplanes and skim over the water and not in it. This means that whereas the liner pushes aside the water and uses enormous power in doing it, the hydroplane floats on the water.

BRAVO QUEEN MARY!
Speed, 1936

At 2.36 a.m. on Monday, August 31st, the Cunard White Star liner *Queen Mary* arrived at Cherbourg after making a record crossing of the Atlantic in less than four days and regaining for Great Britain the coveted Blue Riband previously held by the French liner, *Normandie.* The last British Blue Riband holder was the *Mauretania,* which retained it for over 22 years; longer than any other liner.

Altogether the *Queen Mary* set up six records: fastest crossing West to East, fastest crossing East to West, fastest day's run Westbound, fastest day's crossing Eastbound, fastest port to port passage Cherbourg to New York, fastest port to port passage New York to Cherbourg. The fastest day's run on the outward voyage was made on the second day, when a distance of 760 miles was covered, at an average speed of 30.40 knots an hour. On the return voyage the fastest day's run was made on the third day, a distance of 713 miles being covered at an average speed of exactly 31 knots.

THE OCEAN EXPRESS BREMEN
F. A. Breuhaus de Groot

This powerful organism, constructed according to consequential, clearly defined laws, is a magnificent floating hotel, born of the spirit of modern engineering. The outward aspect of the hull of the ship shows clearly cut, purposeful outlines, unprecedented in beauty and overwhelming as an expression of the technical ideas of the world of 1930. The elegance of the modern automobile, the smartness of the modern express steamer, the gigantic power of a large express train engine, the emphatic pronunciation of the principle of rapid speed in the carrying-out of the general purpose – all this is embodied in the *Bremen* in an admirable manner. Leading engineers have created in this ship a piece of work which in technical as well as artistic respect may serve as a model and is without a precedent. The *Bremen* may be regarded as the most complicated and most magnificent instrument of transport, of the highest workmanship down to the smallest details. The constructive skeleton of this vessel, combined with an interior organism of the highest technical perfection, presents in every detail a work of art. It is a living, though technical, body made of the noblest materials, animated and ruled by the human will, and serving as a connecting

link between the continents. The many excellent qualities of this imposing means of transport are crowned by the maximum of safety and comfort offered to the passengers. Pampered humanity considers all these things a matter of course at our present time. The fundamental task of the builders of the ship, to satisfy the most fastidious passengers, was set not only to all the technical but also to all the artistic collaborators as the basis of their work, and was faithfully adhered to. The brilliant beauty of this achievement of the art of engineering imbues us with admiration for the ingenuity of the builders of the ship. Their ability was not handicapped by the adherence to a particular style, and so their work became an expression of the mentality of progressive mankind.

The task of the collaborating artists was to attain the same climax in their domain. The ocean-steamer is in the first place a floating hotel which must be adapted to the technically computed body of the ship. Adherence to the sea-going qualities must be the self-evident creative basis for the artist. The spatial arrangement excludes the natural sources of light for many of the rooms. This essential question demands an especial study of the most satisfactory and most practical methods of illumination, based on various possibilities of light-sources. In connection therewith, the choice of material, of colours and, last but not least, of the architectonic line play an important role. Utility combined with beauty alone guarantees the perfection of the desired result. The architecture of the Lloyd Express Steamer *Bremen* shows modern German decorative art, and represents a great advance towards the definite style of our time. In order to attain such absolute perfection, the artist must strive to achieve it in his artistic capability, and the passenger must endeavour to develop a desire for such perfection. The ostentatious luxury of former times, which no longer appeals to the man of to-day, has been avoided in the interior decoration of the *Bremen* by laying stress on the purity of form, on the beauty of line and on the superior quality of the material. The architecture of the *Bremen* emancipates us from

a time which is not our own and leads us into the grandeur of our present age, in which we desire to breathe and not to suffocate.

Norddeutscher-Lloyd's initial plans for a new, fast steamer were based on their other large passenger ships. However, war interrupted the company's steamship service until as late as 1924, by which time the comapny needed to make a thorough study not only of modern equipment being offerred by the North-Atlantic passenger service, but also of the standards of living of the people of North America in their newest hotels, apartment houses, etc., since the North Americans are known to make up the principal contingent of the passengers travelling in the first class, which forms the economic backbone of the passenger trade, and especially that of the express service. As far as speed was concerned, this tended towards a further increase, the more so as the possibility for it was given by the perfection of the methods of engine construction. But on long voyages without intermediate ports great speed demands a large hull. Large steamers are, moreover, preferred by the passengers to smaller ships, because the former can more easily overcome the severity of the weather, they can be supplied with more adequate devices to insure safety, and they can also be furnished with more comfort than smaller ships.

The demand for comfort, which has grown extraordinarily since the war, made the creation of modern accommodations necessary

Built for speed: the marked streamlining of the express steamer *Bremen*. A debenture issue, floated in the United States, provided the necessary finance for the liner and in 1929, on her first voyage to America, the *Bremen* put an end to Cunard speed supremacy on the Western ocean. Oil on canvas by Hans Bohrdt.

78

Querschnitt Haupt-Treppenhaus I. Klasse   Cross-Section Principal Staircase I. Class
Professor Fritz August Breuhaus, Düsseldorf

A cross-section of the principal staircase in first class on the *Bremen,* by Prof. Fritz August Breuhaus de Groot. All her staircases kept strictly to the maritime look and the contrast between precious wood and lacquer, partly gilded, provided a most interesting effect. Paintings, light fixtures and mirrors enlivened the surfaces.

79

Vivid colouring arrests the eye of the beholder in these two designs from Prof. Friedrich Heubner of Munich. *Right.* Glass-window "Europe". Eminent German designers competed for the distinction of creating the crack super liner *Bremen*.

in all passenger classes. In place of the former steerage quarters for emigrants and the subsequent primitive cabin arrangement, a third-class cabin accommodation for two or three persons has been provided, such as was once given only to second-class passengers. The cabins for the Second Class, and especially for the Tourist Class and the Third Class, which hitherto were placed on the two decks below the bulkhead deck, and at that chiefly at both ends of the vessel, have wholly disappeared from these parts of the ship. The

cabins of all classes have washstands, wardrobes and other such accommodations desired by the modern traveller.

The fundamental principle observed in the arrangement of the passenger accommodations was their unconditional adaptation to the necessities of the voyage at sea, greatest expediency, comfort and ease for the passengers, the employment of only the very best material, but, on the other hand, in compliance with the tendency of modern art, the avoidance of all superfluous luxury and

Glass-window "The Stadtmusikanten of Bremen". The *Bremen's* interior reflected the revolutionary concepts of German design in the twenties. The lounge was principally decorated with plastics and the age of synthetic materials had arrived.

pompous display. Thus, there originated from the combination of the great experience of the Norddeutscher Lloyd in the passenger service with the standards of living and the increased demand for comfort on the part of the passengers, especially of the Americans, the equipment which is provided today on the *Bremen*. The chief share of the passenger accommodations is required by the First Class, as is a matter of course on a big modern express steamer for which the consideration of rentability must be predominant. The fundamental idea of the technical scheme for this Class was the arrangement of the totality of the cabins into a compact three-storied block, above which a large deck house extends from fore to aft, surrounded on all sides by the broad expanse of the promenade deck, the centre of which is taken up by the long and lofty Lounge of the First Class. The extensive domestic department of the ship made it necessary to group the various dining-rooms and the other rooms devoted to this service as close together as possible. Consequently all

Centre. **First class Smoking Room on the *Bremen,* equipped with leather-covered chairs of dark walnut finished like rosewood. Lockers for games and cigars were built into a wall and the room contained a tarsia-work, representing stages in the development of tobacco.**

Precious objects were on offer in the *Bremen's* Street of Shops. The walls and show cases were covered with pigskin and an illuminated fountain dispensed scent. A Smyrna carpet covered the floor and comfortable chairs invited the shopper to rest.

these rooms and kitchens were arranged on one special deck just below the deck containing the social rooms. In this arrangement, the dining-room of the First Class, with its annexes and its catering department, played the principal role, for this room alone was to have a seating capacity for more than 600 persons.

The gigantic engine and boiler system of the ship, especially the latter, with its immense funnels, essentially influenced the construction of the rooms of the First Class. Thus the boiler-rooms were divided into two principal groups, which division was, besides, desirable for reasons of the safety and the navigability of the vessel. Between these two chief groups of boiler-rooms, the extensive dining-room of the First Class and, above the cabin-section, the large First Class Lounge, found their best and natural location. Both rooms are situated about midships. As a natural development of this arrangement we find in the lowest part of the ship, in the most favourable and quiet location, the Swimming-Pool of the First Class. For the up-and-downward communication between Swimming-Pool, Dining-Room and Lounge serves the big ten-storied main staircase which is located immediately in front of these rooms. At its top, above the huge Lounge, is the airy Roof-Garden Restaurant. For an additional connection between the first-class rooms and the upper deck-house, a second staircase has been provided aft. The remarkable distance between her two short and sturdy funnels, the two masts, harmoniously placed forward and aft, the projecting stem and the so-called cruiser-stern, which in modern times has been adopted by commercial navigation, endow the vessel with her individual and highly impressive outward character.

The Norddeutscher Lloyd resolved to invite the leading German architects to compete for the artistic decoration of the first and second class saloons of the *Bremen,* which had been reserved by contract with the shipyard for the Company's own decision. The artists received, for their artistic elaboration, the technical specifications for the saloons and the staircases in the form of scaled plans and designs, which,

at the same time, contained the principal steel connections of the hull of the ship. Thus it was the closest and most intuitive collaboration of the three factors, artists, engineers and interior decorators, that brought about the creation of the new giant of the Norddeutscher Lloyd.

ITALIAN SHIPPING
Frank C. Bowen

The end of the war in 1918 made an immense difference to Italy at sea, for the country acquired the northern Adriatic coast of the former Austro-Hungarian Empire. This not only encouraged the theory that the Adriatic should be an Italian lake, but also gave to the country a number of well-equipped dockyards, shipbuilding establishments and ports.

Italy did not share in the general distribution of the German Merchant Service in reparation for the submarine campaign. She did far better by taking 213 steamers, totalling nearly 600,000 tons gross, which had formerly been the bulk of the Austro-Hungarian Merchant Service. With the port of Trieste were transferred a number of flourishing shipping companies which had formerly flown the Austrian flag, although they had been largely Italian in their personnel.

In many ways the Fascist regime reversed previous Government policy in dealing with the Merchant Service. It based its first schemes on the fact that shipping should be allowed to work out its own salvation as far as possible, and in the early days shipping was given as much independent control as possible.

Services were divided into two groups, the "indispensable lines" which were those connecting the mainland to the isolated Italian possessions by the shortest route and at the highest speed, and the "useful lines" which connected Italy with foreign ports and were designed to develop trade and emigration. A new subsidy scheme began in 1926, the agreements with the "indispensable lines" being for twenty years and with the "useful lines" for five and ten years. Almost without exception the ships were Italian-built, and as far as possible even the materials were of Italian manufacture.

The shipbuilding industry in Italy suffered from the slump as much as in other countries. As the Government considered shipbuilding to be as important to the country as shipping, measures were also taken to give it every encouragement. Foreign orders, naval and

The *Bremen's* first class swimming pool was filled with pure filtered water when the steamer reached the high seas. Parabolic reflectors provided a therapeutic effect and magnificent illumination. Dressing rooms were concealed from view and only non-rusting metals were used.

A prototype for all fashionable ballrooms, the *Bremen's* Ballroom was divided into a central dancing floor, a stage, boxes and a bar. In the centre of the room an illuminated fountain stood on a floor of glass mosaic. Films were shown every afternoon.

Until 1922 Italy had no passenger liners comparable to those of North West Europe. Ten years on, the Italian government, aiming to attract American tourists to Italy, insisted that rival companies on the Atlantic run combine to form the Italia Line. Mussolini's bid for a share of the Atlantic riches was the record-breaking *Rex*, colossus of the Italian Mercantile marine. Built with government support, her success was widely applauded in the Italian press.

mercantile, were obtained wherever possible, and in this the whole resources of the Government were mobilized. Shipbuilding bounties were established on a complicated system and a large fund was formed to grant loans to shipowners who would otherwise have been unable to pay for new tonnage.

Atlantic Speed Record

The Italian authorities wanted the national flag to have its full place in the sun, and their problem was made more difficult by the indefinite suspension of the emigrant trade to the United States, on which Italian shipping had formerly depended. Undeterred by this suspension, they argued that if they could not get the third-class trade they would have the first-class.

Germany held the Blue Riband of the Atlantic with the *Bremen* and the *Europa* and most of the American holiday-makers were influenced by this to go to Northern Europe at the beginning of their vacation, only taking in the attractions of Italy when their time was as nearly spent as their money. Italy had never before considered either record breakers or giant ships, but she determined to do so at this juncture.

The three principal Italian concerns interested in the North and South American trade were the Navigazione Generale Italiana, the Lloyd Sabaudo and the Cosulich Lines. These three companies were in as healthy a competition with one another as keen shipping companies generally are.

The authorities decided to stop this. The Italian Merchant Service was fighting foreign competition and it must do so with a united front. The three companies must sink their differences and run as a single concern. Then the Government would give them every assistance in building ships big and fast enough to gain the Blue Riband for Italy for the first time in its history, and to attract the most fastidious of American travellers.

So the Italia Line came into being in 1932 as an amalgamation of the three companies. In the following year the Board, which had been formed on the scale usual with such

amalgamations, was drastically cut down and seven practical directors took the place of twenty-one.

The *Rex* and the *Conte Di Savoia* were built in Italian yards. The vessels had gross tonnages of 51,062 and of 48,502 respectively. Some initial trouble was caused when judgments of experienced shipping men, who were running the company, were overruled. In August 1934, however, the *Rex* won the Blue Riband in dashing style and, until it was taken from Italy by France with the liner *Normandie,* the *Rex* and her sister secured the best of the American holiday traffic. To a country which regards tourists as a major industry, this was everything that could be desired.

The Italia Line is the most important concern, now embracing the Lloyd Triestino as well as the original companies. It runs services to New York, South America, South Africa, Australia, India and the Far East. Its tonnage will bear comparison with that of any of its rivals, and it has an excellent reputation with passengers. The Navigazione Libera Triestina runs to South Africa, Central America, West Africa and the North Pacific. The Adria Line maintains many services between Italy and other countries in Europe. The minor companies are kept in a high state of efficiency, perhaps largely by fear of the consequences.

THE REX AND THE CONTE DI SAVOIA
A. P. Le M. Sinkinson

There is between the North American continent and Europe, an important service which is not primarily concerned with the seaports of northern Europe. New York and Naples are connected by a direct express steamer service maintained by two of the most up-to-date liners operating to-day. They are the *Rex* and the *Conte di Savoia,* of the Italia Line.

These vessels are speedy as well as modern, for both have broken records and the *Rex* has held the Blue Riband of the Atlantic. The Italia Line is an amalgamation of several important concerns, including the Navigazione Generale Italiana, the Cosulich Line and the Lloyd

Sabauda. Its record-breakers are the largest vessels in an extensive fleet.

The route taken by the *Rex* and her sister involves the crossing of the Atlantic from New York to Gibraltar, or *vice-versa*. Two calls are made in the Mediterranean before the liner reaches the end of her voyage at Naples. These are at Nice, on the French Riviera, and at Genoa, on the fringe of the Italian Riviera.

Thus the service is especially attractive to those Americans who respond to the appeal of this enchanting part of the Mediterranean coast, as well as to those who are irresistibly drawn by the lure of Italy. Apart, however, from the tourist and seasonal trade, there is a constant and important business trade. As large numbers of Italians live in or have business with the United States the value of the link will be appreciated. The voyage between New York and Genoa is made in six and a half days.

The *Rex,* elder of the two vessels, was built by the Ansaldo Yard at Sestri Ponente, in the Gulf of Genoa, and was completed in 1932. The designed speed is 27.1 knots, but the *Rex* has proved herself capable of a considerably faster rate.

The *Conte di Savoia* has many points of resemblance to the *Rex,* but she is not identical in design. Launched on October 28, 1931, by H.R.H. Princess Maria of Piedmont, the younger ship was built by the United Adriatic Shipyards at Trieste, the famous seaport at the head of the Adriatic.

Her designed speed is the same as that of the *Rex.* In May 1933 she secured the westbound record from Gibraltar to the Ambrose Light, New York. She held this record until August 1934, when it was taken from her by the *Rex.*

An exclusive feature of the *Conte di Savoia* is the provision of a stabilizer. This device has been adopted for the first time in a large passenger liner. The stabilizer in the *Conte di Savoia* consists of three gyroscopes, of the Sperry type, of equal dimensions. Each gyroscope has a fly-wheel weighing 176 tons and making 910 revolutions s minute. The total weight of the stabilizer is 750 tons, and the horse-power absorbed is 2,000. It is claimed that, with the stabilizer in operation, the vessel will not roll more than five degrees (two and a half degrees to either side) even in the roughest weather. Those who are afraid to take a sea voyage for fear of sea-sickness should therefore have no qualms about booking a passage on the vessel.

Class Distinction

At first four classes were provided in either vessel – first class, special class, tourist class and third class, but now the special class has been merged in the tourist class. The term "special class" may sound a little mystifying; but its adoption was due to an almost universal prejudice on the part of the travelling public.

There are few people who do not regard the expression "second-class" as a term of disparagement. Mediocrity may be golden, but it is certainly uninspiring. Shipping companies are fighting shy of second class. The Italia Line evolved a brilliant substitute for the hated denomination, and special-class passengers took pride in accommodation for which second-class passengers might have made excuses. Now that special-class accommodation is available for tourist-class passengers in either vessel, the tourist-class passenger in the *Rex* or *Conte di Savoia* is particularly well served.

It is interesting to examine the make-up of the Chief Purser's staff. That of the *Rex* will serve as an example. The average landsman seems to think that a liner's staff consists mainly of stewards. Most passengers find the services of a steward invaluable when they are well and indispensable when they are under the weather. There is therefore some excuse for their pre-occupation. In spite of this, the total number of stewards and stewardesses in the *Rex* – 164 – is less than half the total of the Chief Purser's staff. There are two head waiters and two assistant head waiters. Six barmen need the assistance of 112 assistants. Coffee is so important in an Italian liner that there are four "coffee-cooks". Eleven musicians provide the personnel for the ship's orchestra.

Passengers who are particular about their clothes will be glad to hear that there are

three wardrobe keepers, a tailor's presser, a laundryman and three women starchers and ironers.

Hairdressing and its cognate crafts are in the hands of two ladies' hairdressers, five barbers and one manicurist. A miscellaneous list of trades includes two gymnasium stewards, two photographers and three printers. The printers produce the ship's newspaper, the *Corriere del Mare* ("Sea Post"), which is a daily publication. Finally, there are fifteen firemen to deal with any emergency in their sphere.

The kitchen staff, under a chef assisted by a second chef, amounts to eighty-nine. There are thirty-one cooks and five pastry cooks, an ice-cream maker, a cellarman, two butchers, five provision storekeepers, six bakers, and no fewer than thirty-six washers-up.

Lido in the Atlantic

On the *Conte di Savoia* the scheme of decoration is particularly fine, being the work of the Italian architect Gustavo Pulitzer Finali, of Trieste.

The Sun Deck gives access to a large open-air swimming pool, flanked by wide terraces and gangways. The Sports Deck contains the bridge, forward, the chart room, the wireless station, and the appropriately named Lido. Here are other entrances to the swimming pool, the Lido Café and Restaurant, and the shooting gallery. This deck, except for a small section at the after end and at a lower level, is reserved for first-class passengers.

In the forward end of the Promenade Deck is a belvedere, so called because it commands an uninterrupted view of the sea, Between the funnels is a veranda. The Grand Open-Air Promenade extends all round the deck. On the Promenade Deck also are eight veranda suites and some first-class staterooms. There is a fully-equipped gymnasium, with an adjoining Roman bath. On this deck are some of the ship's boats, the Commander's cabin, and various offices.

The Social Deck is one of the most important in the ship. Right forward is another belvedere. Next to this is the Winter Garden and, behind it, the Club, with bar and dance floor. From the two entrances to the Winter Garden there extends aft, on either side of the vessel, the Enclosed Veranda. It is protected from the weather by glass screens. Leading aft from the Club, on the port side. are the card room and, on the starboard side, the Princess Gallery, giving access to the lounge, foyer and writing room.

We now reach the most striking feature of the ship – the Grand Colonna Hall. Although elsewhere in the ship the keynote of the decorations is modern, the claims of the antique have not been forgotten here. The Grand Colonna Hall is named after the famous gallery of the Colonna Palace in Rome, dating from 1620 and incorporating ancient Roman marble and sculptures. The hall is divided into a nave and two aisles. On the ceiling is a reproduction of the painting in the Colonna Gallery, by Lucchesini, of the battle of Lepanto.

The apartment is decorated with a profusion of marble pilasters, classical sculptures, friezes and cornices in the style of the seventeenth century. In the hall is a bronze bust by Marlya Lednicka of H.R.H. Princess Maria of Piedmont, sponsor to the vessel. The total floor area of the Grand Colonna Hall is 5,918 square feet and its height is 24 feet. The central space is reserved for dancing. Opening out of the hall are the first-class buffet-bar and the Chapel. Although the Chapel is situated in the first-class part of the ship, it is accessible to passengers of all classes. In the after end of the Social Deck are the first-class Winter Swimming Pool, with a gymnasium and bar adjoining, and the Sports Deck, tourist class, with a dais for fencing and boxing.

THE STEWARDESS NURSE
The Queen

The Stewardess on board is nearly always a kindly and obliging woman. She often shows a degree of tenderness and human sympathy with women and children under disagreeable circumstances which can excite nothing but gratitude ,and respect in those to whom she ministers. Occasionally, like the noble woman whose sacrifice of her own life for the sake of

The Greek Line, based at Piraeus, was established in 1937 with the departure from that port of the *Nea Hellas,* an ex-Anchor Line steamer, bound for New York. The practice of buying unwanted passenger liners and refitting them for further employment, with primarily tourist-class accommodation, originated with the Greek Line.

the passengers in the *Stella* is commemorated in a monument at Southampton, a stewardess has risen to the height of heroism. The stewardess generally does her utmost; and the captain himself can do no more. But she has not had, like the captain, any special training for her duties.

Steamship companies are too apt to regard the post of stewardess as an appointment for bestowal on a woman related to some member of their crew. The idea that a man's widow or daughter will be provided with a comfortable berth as stewardess is thought to make the service of passenger vessels more attractive.

By making the post of stewardess a kind of perquisite for female relations of the crew, the companies hope to enlist the services of a superior class of men. But it must be remembered that a large proportion of the salary of the stewardess comes out of the pockets of the women passengers in the form of tips. So that, if we do not shrink from uncomfortable conclusions, we shall find, that the women passengers are getting the services of an indifferently trained or untrained stewardess, in order that the company may get an efficient crew on cheaper terms, or, in fact, that tips to the stewardess go indirectly to eke out the crew's wages. The cost and the profits of transport have, of course, to be defrayed by the passengers in any case; it is only this system of indirect and circuitous payment which is objectionable.

An effort is being made to induce companies to choose stewardesses who are specially qualified for the performance of their duties and a knowledge of nursing is being insisted upon. The *Daily Mail,* the *British Medical Journal,* and the *Hospital* have all recently expressed themselves in this sense, and the last mentioned paper says it is proposed to form an association of women nurses for the use of vessels whose owners may desire to employ them. It should hardly be necessary to point out how great is the likelihood of passengers falling ill at sea. Not only must sea-sickness itself be considered, with all the complications to which, in the case of delicate people it may give rise, but there is a possibility

of almost every other kind of physical mischance occurring. It is highly unlikely that, among a large company of passengers making a voyage of perhaps many days or weeks, all should remain from start to finish in sound health. The probability is that there will be some few cases of serious illness, many of minor maladies, and there may even be an epidemic disease. The ship's doctor will, of

course, be in attendance, but he cannot be expected to nurse the patients nor to give an ignorant stewardess her training at the passengers' expense. A strong case, we submit, exists for the appointment of stewardesses who have had some hospital training, and whose chief qualification is not that they are related to the crew or the company, but that they are intelligent, educated women, thoroughly capable of performing any of the nursing duties that are likely to present themselves.

FRENCH PLANNING AND DECORATION
P. De Malglaive, 1937

A ship is the result of a stupendous amount of compromises. Even before the first pencil line is drawn by the draughtsmen, compromises must already have been reached, and as the ship's design takes more definite shape, the problems to be solved by mutual agreement increase in number and importance. On one side, omnipotent, masterful, and dictatorial, true personifications of Almighty God in His realm, are the naval architects, who think only of weight, stresses, resistance to propulsion, floodability, watertight bulkheads, fireproof screens, and other paramount problems, and who have very definite views as to what they want done; on the other, there are the marine engineers, who want space, weight, and more space and weight, for their boilers and engines. Then there is the passenger manager, who asks

In Northern Waters: passage fares, for 1898, for summer excursions to Norway and elsewhere. By 1910 the Norwegians were looking eastwards and the Norwegian America Line, financially endorsed by their government, was founded.

for cabins as big as ballrooms, public rooms like cathedrals, and a very large passenger-carrying capacity as well; the freight manager suggests discreetly, but in no uncertain manner, that it would be useful to have big cargo-carrying capacity, with, of course, large refrigerated space. At the very last minute the catering department has the bright idea that boiler and engine-room space should be allotted to its staff and equipment, as good food is the paramount item aboard. Most important of all is the owner, who wants to spend the smallest possible amount of money, or none at all if possible, but expects any vessel to be without fuel or upkeep bills, running always to schedule, never needing any lay-up and in any season filled to capacity with passengers and earning 100 per cent returns.

The ingenuity of countless Solomons would be taxed to the utmost to find a middle way between these legitimate but conflicting requirements, but found it must be. So in the case of such a liner as the *Normandie,* which by her size alone would not fail to attract universal attention, we felt justified in hoping that the achievement would be enhanced by enlisting the aid of our land architects and artists in her design.

It would be a very great error to believe, as some seem to have believed, that in designing the ship the architects were allowed the slightest liberty with the work of the naval architects and engineers, who always had the final word as, before anything else, a ship will always be a ship.

A few words on the external appearance of the ship, to which much time has been devoted, our aim having been to give her excellent seaworthiness coupled with a feeling of strength, power and beauty. To achieve these ends, the collaboration of M. Pacon has been invaluable. All *impedimenta* have been removed and put in their proper place; decks have been cleared entirely, by proper arrangements, of any visible gear which could mar the ship's lines, impede her action or be in the way of passengers.

We are far from claiming to have produced a masterpiece of eternal fame, but do feel that in

Streamlining to the limit: the St. Nazaire masterpiece, *Normandie*. The turbo-electric drive system was unique among record-breakers and much of the auxiliary machinery was novel. The quality of her fittings has never been equalled. Behaviour in bad weather (the Atlantic can be one of the worst passages) was exemplary and the pronounced sheer forward reduced pitching to a minimum.

90

Cie Gle TRANSATLANTIQUE

French Line

NORMANDIE

LONGITUDINAL SECTION

S/S NORMANDIE

the race to perfection we have perhaps laid a modest milestone on that great road of progress along which we all strive so valiantly towards our distant goal. We hope that our toil and cares, nevertheless, have not been fruitless, and that our ship is a fitting monument to modern shipbuilding and architectural ingenuity, as conceived by my compatriots.

A further point is that in this ship the decorators have not "gone modern," and yet I think she is quite "contemporary." In certain countries – we are not the only country – people are apt suddenly to "go modern," just as some go wild and others go mad. In France, it always seems to me, they *grow* modern, and growing presupposes that they are rooted in some soil, and that branches and twigs are part and parcel of the same tree. I think the main impression one gets in regard to the *Normandie's* decoration is that it has grown out of French tradition, but has been thoroughly adapted to present-day needs and requirements, making use of all the materials and methods.

It is a curious fact that all these big passenger ships seem to tend to accentuate their national characteristics, whether we look at the *Normandie*, the *Queen Mary*, the *Europa* or the Italian and Dutch ships. There is a definite national tinge about them which is very refreshing and which relieves the monotony of a too international world.

P. DE MALGLAIVE,
Resident Director in England of the
Compagnie Générale Transatlantique.

THE FLOATING PALACE FROM FRANCE
American Architect, 1935

The S.S. *Normandie* – which weighs 70,000 tons and is almost as long as the Empire State Building is high – is an uncanny achievement for which the French have become famous. The speed of the ship and all of its mechanical devices constitute in themselves a major miracle even in this age. But aside from these,

the *Normandie* is unique as a travelling exhibit of native art and industrial design. Thus she is as truly noteworthy as any exposition acclaimed in Paris.

To fit this ship the foremost designers in France were given free rein. It is strikingly obvious that no expense, imagination or materials have been spared. And if, to American designers, the results are too florid, too sumptuously grand, let them remember that the labours of the architects – M.M. Bîuwens de Boijen, Expert, Patout and Pacon – have made them "typically French".

In former times the work of French architects has not gone entirely unnoticed by American designers. Hardly an American countryside exists that cannot boast of Normandy cottages or of grand houses designed under the "inspiration" of the chateaux. And on almost every main street one can see the floriated facades begotten by the 1925 Paris Exposition.

But even without regard to its embryonic influence on design, the *Normandie* is notable in at least two practical instances. First, it is the most completely fire-proofed vessel ever launched. Second, in the wide variety of materials that have been employed there exist techniques that could undoubtedly be applied with excellent results to the solution of many American problems of decorative design and construction.

As to the first of these, the *Normandie's* owners have taken every presently known precaution to prevent that greatest of maritime horrors – fire. Structurally the boat is divided into compartments – 321 of them – each separated by partitions that are as fireproof as modern science can make them. These are of several types, all equally efficient. One, for example – called "type A" – is built of studs covered with asbestos, two thicknesses of rock wool and a thick sheet of steel. Though its total thickness is only about 5 inches, this construction is said to resist for 20 minutes a temperature of 1500° F.

But construction is not alone sufficient to eliminate the fire hazard. Consequently, an equal amount of preventive care has been

lavished upon finishes. In many instances finish materials are inherently non-inflammable. Witness to this is the fact that much glass and metal has been used for wall facings. Wood – used extensively as both finish and furniture – has been treated chemically so that it will not support combustion and the same sort of treatment has been given to other naturally inflammable wall coverings and to decorative fabrics in all rooms, public or private. Strictly speaking, of course, all these have not been rendered completely fireproof. Even "fireproof wood" will burn if subjected to steady and intense heat. But in that the chemicals used in their treatment will not feed flames, the fire hazard has been reduced so that it is now regarded as a factor of minor importance. Even the paint was composed with special ingredients to withstand temperatures up to 750° F. And as an additional safeguard, the entire ship is controlled by the most elaborate and delicate mechanical system for fire detection ever installed.

This insistence upon firesafeness undoubtedly had some influence upon the choice of materials in the *Normandie*. In the largest public rooms – the Main Hall, Dining Room and Lounge – glass and some marble were chiefly used. Walls of the former are Algerian onyx, copper and glass; and in the Dining Room, embossed cast glass panels cover most of the wall surfaces. In the Main Lounge, also, walls are lined with glass, painted and etched with designs that depict the story of navigation from its earliest beginnings.

This extensive use of glass in various forms and finishes has made possible, in many instances, unusual methods of lighting. But other materials have been used with the same degree of ingenuity if not to the same extent. Thus, in the Smoking Room, wall panels are completely covered in brown-red *coromandel* lacquer. They are the work of Jean Dunand and his two sons, specialists in lacquer, an ancient material that changes density with the weather and involves an exhausting technique in its application. It is usually applied over wood or a base built up with layers of resin, canvas, sawdust, wood and earth. Panels in the

Normandie's smoking room, however, have a base of a fireproof plastic developed by the Dunands and said to be more susceptible to carving or modelling than any of the more usual matt-lacquer bases. Finishing of such panels required extreme care. It is partly accomplished by polishing with pumice and charcoal, but final touches are given by rubbing with only the palm of the hand.

In other public rooms, and in some staterooms, pigskin and parchment have been used for wall surfacing. And the walls of many staterooms are covered with stainless steel and aluminum. These materials are regarded as experiments. So far as is known, this is the first time such materials have been used for wall finishes of the living quarters aboard a passenger liner. The installations on the *Normandie*, therefore, should serve the double purpose of giving to French Line technicians valuable information as to corrosion-resisting qualities of the metals thus used, and also inform them of the reactions of passengers to metal-lined rooms.

On the average passenger's reaction to most of the first class rooms, officials need speculate but little. Those who buy first class pay their premium for magnificence, and on the *Normandie* there is certainly no dearth of this. In most of the public spaces, size alone is one contribution to a lavish, formal splendour. The Main Lounge, for example, is 105 x 75 ft.: and the Dining Room, 300 ft. in length, extends three decks in height, as does the Main Hall, which measures 70 x 66 ft.

Modernity characterizes the design of most spaces throughout the ship, though a few private rooms are done in traditional styles. To many, the results may be personally distasteful. There are those who will consider them too bizarre, too lacking in the functional simplicity of another school of French design headed by Le Corbusier, Lurcat and Mallet-Stevens. On the other hand, even more, probably, will condemn the *Normandie's* interiors because they conform to no accepted precedent of architecture or decoration. It is precisely this unorthodox quality about the boat – from her turbo-electric power plant to her mahogany-

inlaid decks – that makes the work of her designers worthy of interest on the part of American architects. Within her the most vaunted of French craftsmen have paraded the superlatives of their several abilities. A huge floating palace – France's $59,000,000 bid to maritime leadership and a seagoing exhibition of her contemporary art.

NORMANDIE
Oliver P. Bernard

Invited to travel on biggest, fastest, most luxurious passenger steamship afloat. So excited by prospect of another marine adventure, forgot my passport, Newhaven passport officials were kind, advised me as architect to get my foundations right next time. The Channel not so kind to bad sailors aboard torpedo-bitten packet *Rouen;* had her nose bitten off 1916. Some day we'll build twenty-one span viaduct between Shakespeare Cliff and Bris Nez, make England hemispheric centre of the globe. Toll on mechanical transport will pay its way; no ventilating nor pumping problems involved; in war-time a wad of gun-cotton severs connections until armistice if necessary. That bridge will be gilt-edged investment for G.B. and soundest link in League of Nations.

Pacified passport official in Dieppe with letter of invitation from Compagnie Générale Transatlantique. First time in Havre since war; they've built fine railway station since then; some day England may have one too, accidentally showing visitors some progress since an architect worshipped his own work at St. Pancras. Seaports are not architectural. My travelling companion baulked at exploring sailors' quarters in Havre; the smell of them, red lights for mariners, mussels, music, so alluring, but companion obdurate: no place for respectable publisher.

Next morning discovered magnificent wharf built by the French Line, beside that, the champion heavyweight of the seven seas with steam up for second round trip to New York: pride of great nation, *chef-d'oeuvre* of French art and engineering – which ever comes first?

(American Institute of Civil Engineers maintains that good engineers must be artists.) Gold standard and constitution of Republique political sideshows compared with the *paquebot Normandie:* Chamber of Deputies may prostitute own honour, but not so the genius and integrity which assembles 160,000 horse-power to plough wind and wave, with over 3,300 beings, logging about 800 knots per day. Went aboard thousand-foot masterpiece of marine engineering. This travelling exhibition of industrial art reaches New York before passengers can see it all: I have seven hours to digest latest accomplishments of master craftsmen of France; no time to peep at what I want to see most of all: turbines that do 2,400 revolutions to the minute, making four propellers spin like tops, each one bearing 40,000 thrusting horse-power.

Prepared for shock in main Entrance Hall, and got it; golden onyx from Algeria, ashlar by the metre, tons of it, 50,000 kilos, pick of the quarries; untrammelled walls of frozen sunshine. No country handles marble like France. Artificial light in mass formation of glass from St. Gobain. Let me weep for such glass products from St. Helens.

The Grand Saloon, or Lounge, presents Jean Dupas as triumphant etcher, draughtsman, and painter on glass. But somebody's wife or daughter must have chosen the furniture and fumbled with the carpet; murder of what should be the grandest saloon afloat or ashore.

Fumoir, the smoke room, in gilt metal and gorgeous lacquer, is a dream from Arabian Nights; coloured splendour heaped on hammered gold, oriental vision, consummate design and craftsmanship: profoundly delighted once again to recognise magnificent work of Jean Dunand, greatest decorator in France. Alas, and again, who the ... chose the furniture?

Down below, they call it *Le Hall Superior;* so it is, but not so sure that ironmaster Subes has quite done the trick with his metal lift cages. Maybe they rushed him. And the lighting, too? Building goes smoothly enough as a rule, but there's generally a squabble over *décor;* the French hurry it, while we dally with

the R.A. and Who's Who! Hence, the French make some mistakes and we are often so confoundedly dull.

The Grand Dining Saloon fully deserves its title; seats seven hundred or more in the grand manner; if it serves so many equally well, must have the most wonderful service and kitchen ever designed for first-class meals. A crystal palace roofed with solid gold; glass illuminated and otherwise – suspect the otherwise not quite as purposed; seems unsafe, but effect is extraordinary: walls like curtains of frosted lace. Eight private dining saloons, port and starboard of main saloon, suggest settings for short episodes by George Moore: this ship will surely break all records of Atlantic Romance!

Everywhere combination of lighting and ventilating units bears out my own humble pioneering of dual systems at the Cumberland Hotel and elsewhere. It seems, however, that sculpture and *bas-relief* must happen in the best surroundings. Here they lack distinction as usual, except one by Delamarre which is something above hackneyed allegory of Normandy. Decorative sculpture must have distinction or nothing: early Romanesque carvers realized this dictum first and better than any since the twelfth century.

The Cinema is truly first-class vehicle of entertainment, perfect model of what sub-contractors are incapable of doing for those architects who pretend to design cinemas in England. On the other hand, the Chapel is more like the average theatre, not to be scoffed at though it lacks reverence and discourages meditation: designers must believe in what they do and what they do it for!

The Grill Room is a gorgeous sun parlour; highballs and high jinks in an oceanic road house, towering above the sea. The finest situation aboard this leviathan, but not the steadiest. Once more, the furniture made me angry: so many astute persons know the price of everything and the value of nothing!

Walked through *le Jardin d'Hiver*. I love an honest conservatory but despise horticultural affectations described as winter gardens; they're usually so wintry and terribly depressing to plant life, to say nothing of birds and unhappy goldfish. Must hurry up, we're getting near the Solent.

The Swimming Bath does not impress me as much as our own at the Bath Club; water without sunshine is dead; those who've tried waterfalls in the theatre know that. Have walked miles and miles since breakfast: future leviathans must have electric railway service to all parts; in such longitudinal dimensions lifts play no part at all. What? You like exercise. Oh, boy, just see the decks of this Atlantic Playground! Remind one of aerodromes; get me a hammock steward, I'll sleep before the mast and see the sun rise over the edge of this ocean prairie.

Cabins and staterooms far better and much cheaper than so-called "luxury flats" in Park Lane; liners of this calibre will establish the habit of living at sea, away from petrol fumes, hoardings, murderous traffic, hideous shopfronts, and noise, noise, noise; even children happy in wonderful nurseries. As for servant problems, where in this muddled world can there be greater courtesy and finer cuisine than aboard this floating province of France?

Arrived in the Solent at 6 p.m., and lay there for four hours while passports were examined. Some day liners will cross the Atlantic quicker than passengers get their passports stamped and baggage chalked.

R.M.S. QUEEN MARY
Fortune Magazine, 1936

A few days after these words are in print a solid, dark Welshman named Llewellyn, Roberts will undergo the most profound experience of his thirty-two-year career of seafaring. Mr. Roberts, wearing a blue uniform with four gold stripes on the sleeve, will be aboard the Royal Mail Steamer *Queen Mary*, westbound from Southampton on her maiden voyage across the North Atlantic. He will have very little time for jollying the passengers and distinguished deadheads at his table in the dining room, for most of his waking hours he will spend between his office far down on F Deck and the engine rooms below. Mr. Roberts will be fully preoccupied with the

readings on a profusion of dials and gauges, the reports of some fifty junior assistants, the precise pitch of the pervading hums and screams of his machinery. Mr. Llewellyn Roberts is Chief Engineer of R.M.S. *Queen Mary* and is individually responsible for the performance of the greatest power plant afloat. At a word of command from Commodore Sir Edgar Theopilus Britten on the bridge ten decks above, Chief Engineer Roberts must be ready to direct the full power of 200,000 horses in the form of steam pressure, through turbines and gear-wheels and steel shafts to the four bronze propellers that can drive the 80,000-ton ship through the water at the prodigious speed of thirty-four knots. And at the press of a button by some uninteresting passenger on B Deck, Mr. Roberts's machinery must provide the electric current that rings the bell for the steward and pumps the water and freezes the ice cubes and toasts the canapes that go with the passenger's spot of Scotch.

The passenger's highball and the children's electric train and the stout lady's Turkish bath are important in their way, but Mr. Roberts's principal concern is propulsion of a 1,018-foot liner. And to start that process his fabulous world below the waterline includes four large (eighty by sixty feet) boiler rooms, which are as clean and cool as a modern dairy but without any smell. In each room is a unit of six water tube boilers. Every day at sea the unit gulps 150,000 gallons of water – water that must be so carefully purified and softened (lest mineral deposits clog the 6,500 tubes in each boiler) that the mere act of splitting the feed line will set off an automatic alarm. To boil the water into steam there are fifty bunkers full of furnace oil – 8,300 tons in all. From the bunkers the oil is pumped into settling tanks, heated, filtered, heated again until fluid enough to make a fine spray in the 168 burner-nozzles where it becomes a series of white-hot jets within the boiler. For the most efficient combustion, air is forced into the open stokehold by blower fans, developing such a cyclonic draft within the boiler rooms that men are obliged to pass through a double-doored air lock upon entering or leaving. All

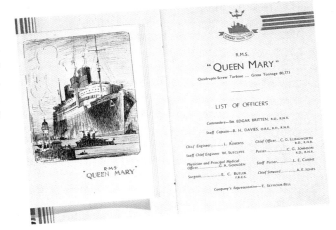

boilers are covered with asbestos, and all pipes, pumps, and open spaces are enamelled white to show the slightest trace of stain, for stain means a leak, and a leak might mean fire.

Steam from the boilers, at 400 pounds pressure and superheated to 700° fahrenheit, is piped aft to two turbine rooms, where its tremendous, bursting energy is harnessed to the task of turning four gearwheels fourteen feet in diameter. The harness is called a turbine. It operates like a hermetically-sealed windmill, only in place of wind there is steam blasting out of flared nozzles, and instead of big vanes there are tiny blades – 257,000 blades in the sixteen turbines of the *Queen Mary*, each blade tested and fitted by hand. The *Queen Mary's* turbines are "four-stage",

Doris Zinkeisen, photographed by Yevonde aboard the *Queen Mary,* 1936. Doris and her sister Anna painted decorative panels for the ship's interior. This column was in the verandah grill, a night club on the sun deck. Walled by twenty two adjustable windows, lights changed with the music, mirrors illuminated dancing feet, and tables were arranged on black-carpeted terraces railed by balustrades of silver, bronze and gold.

Inset. The Tourist Lounge, *Queen Mary.* The *Queen Mary* commanded a special place in the hearts of travellers from all passenger classes.

96

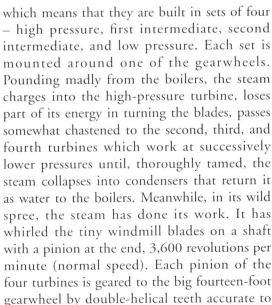

which means that they are built in sets of four – high pressure, first intermediate, second intermediate, and low pressure. Each set is mounted around one of the gearwheels. Pounding madly from the boilers, the steam charges into the high-pressure turbine, loses part of its energy in turning the blades, passes somewhat chastened to the second, third, and fourth turbines which work at successively lower pressures until, thoroughly tamed, the steam collapses into condensers that return it as water to the boilers. Meanwhile, in its wild spree, the steam has done its work. It has whirled the tiny windmill blades on a shaft with a pinion at the end, 3,600 revolutions per minute (normal speed). Each pinion of the four turbines is geared to the big fourteen-foot gearwheel by double-helical teeth accurate to

one-half of one-thousandth of an inch. So the big wheel, fifteen times greater than the pinions in circumference, turns over 240 times a minute. From this gearwheel a hollow steel shaft 27 ⅜ inches in diameter extends aft, penetrates the stern of the hull, and holds at its outboard end a thirty-five-ton propeller, nearly twenty feet in diameter. The propeller and its three mates at the ends of the other tail shafts beat the water with such force as to set up an earsplitting din within the hull, warp the blades perceptibly out of line, and push R.M.S. *Queen Mary,* with 2,000 passengers, across the sea in four days – faster than any other liner afloat.

For seeing to the behaviour of those four bronze screws, Mr. Llewellyn Roberts is paid something like $6,000 a year. (His captain, Sir Edgar Britten, gets not much more.) But his responsibilities do not end there, for there remain to be taken care of such unrelated objects as the gyroscopic compass, the Everlasting Light in the synagogue on B Deck, and the electric ham cooker in the kitchen. So, between the boiler rooms in the lower hold are two steam turbine plants generating electric power for every piece of mechanism on the ship except the propellers. The larger plant provides current for the force-draft fans, lubricating oil pumps, water pumps, condenser, etc., in the engine room, and for the steering gear that swings the 140-ton rudder. The smaller plant, located well forward, is less vital to the *Queen Mary's* locomotion but essential to the business of operating her to any sensible purpose. From it, through 4,000 miles of wire, goes current to light 30,000 lamps; to keep the gyroscopic compass spinning and the repeaters ticking at their stations; to keep the Sperry Iron Mike faithful at the helm and the telltale course recorder squiggling the ship's trail on a roll of paper; to pump the water into the two swimming pools and touch off the steam siren whose note can be heard ten miles; to operate the radio equipment (thirty-two wave lengths, two ship-to-shore telephone channels, equipment for broadcasts from shipboard) and the electric horses in the gymnasium; to heat the crow's-nest for the lookout and work the submarine echo sounder on the bridge; to warm the diesel engine oil for quick starting in the twenty-four powered lifeboats and wipe the wheelhouse window clear of sleet; to hoist the anchor and scour the kitchen knives; to make the coloured lights change in the ballroom and shoot carbon-dioxide gas into a corner of the hold where the smoke detector on the bridge shows fire; to print the ship's newspaper and condition the air in the dining room; to close a watertight bulkhead door by the press of a button on the bridge, and curl a passenger's hair.

Thus from Chief Engineer Llewellyn Roberts's monstrous plant flows the energy that makes R.M.S. *Queen Mary* a thing alive – and thus, from Sir Edgar Britten's bridge, is that energy directed to make the *Queen Mary* behave as a superliner should and indulge the whims of the passengers. Heart and nerve centre, the two organs are housed in the strongest, heaviest body that the shipbuilders of the River Clyde could devise. With her conventional blade bow and cruiser stern, the *Queen Mary* is a classic example of British conservatism. She is not the longest ship in the world (the *Normandie* is eleven feet longer) but she rides down in the water with the heaviest displacement tonnage and the longest waterline measurement (1,004 feet compared to the *Normandie's* 61). She is all foundation; her architects didn't yield an inch in favour of the decorators. And if she is vaguely unexciting to look at, she is still such a magnificent vessel that the Britisher can afford the supreme conceit of Anglo-Saxon understatement: "Yes – she's a good sound job".

Public property

The individual Britisher's pride in the *Queen Mary* is peculiarly personal, because as a taxpayer he has a definite stake in her. The British Government to date has advanced $22,500,000 on account of the *Queen Mary* ($15,000,000 directly toward the $30,000,000 cost of building her; $7,500,000 as working capital for the merged Cunard-White Star Line). There will be more money advanced in the future, perhaps $1,000,000 a year for carrying the mails, and indirect subsidies in the form of low interest and insurance rates.

There were two prime reasons for the government's financing the *Queen Mary*, when Cunard in 1931 found itself unable to see it through alone. One reason was that Great Britain was plainly on her way to losing her top-flight position as a North Atlantic passenger carrier. She had laid down not a single new big ship since the *Aquitania* in 1913. Meanwhile, in France, the *Paris* and the *Ile de France* slid down the ways and the fabulous *Normandie* was started. Germany launched her superliners *Bremen* and *Europa*, Italy her flashy *Rex* and *Conte di Savoia*. Even

Finishing touches, photographed aboard the *Queen Mary* by Yevonde, 1936. The *moderne* bar, in steel, red and cream, was notably fancy for tourist passengers. The ship's designers eschewed the Victorian in their extensive use of glass for light and decoration.

the United States's comparatively small cabin ships, *Manhattan* and *Washington,* were giving Britain's aging monsters unpleasant competition. And the Blue Ribbon for fastest crossing, held for most of twenty-two years by the *Mauretania,* was grabbed away in 1929 by the *Bremen* and passed in turn to the *Europa, Rex,* and *Normandie.*

The second circumstance making the *Queen Mary* a symbol of national resurgence was internal – chronic unemployment in the shipbuilding industry and mean poverty along Scotland's Clydebank. The *Queen Mary* gave jobs, for a while, to some 7,000 workers (average for entire contract, 3,000) and patronage to 572 concerns supplying materials and equipment for the ship. This was the big political issue involved in the stoppage of construction (for lack of funds) and the resumption nearly three years later with government backing. Thus the *Queen Mary,* besides being an international gesture, became a sort of public works project.

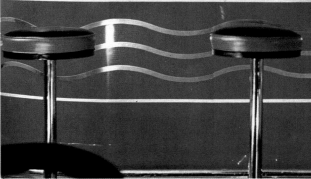

Like public-works projects everywhere, she must submit to a measure of bitter scorn. She has been called unsound; a white elephant; Britain's boondoggle. Among those British subjects concerned less with symbolism and the business of Britannia ruling the waves than with balance sheets, there are some who insist it is a simple arithmetical impossibility for the *Queen Mary* to earn her keep. Many of the factors in the cost and profit equation are secrets of the Cunard-White Star line.

But shipbuilding and ship operation are sciences thoroughly explored, and allowing for fallibility of guesses and the glib approximation of estimates, indications are that the *Queen Mary* might break even if she succeeded in making a 50 per cent average load.

DUTCH SHIPPING
Frank C. Bowen

The Dutch were the first European shipowners to send a steamer across the Atlantic. She was a little vessel of 438 tons, built at Dover in 1826 as the *Calpé* and intended for the short sea

trades. As soon as she was completed the Dutch Navy bought her, renamed her *Curaçao* and used her to carry passengers, mails and special cargo between Holland and the West Indian colony of Curaçao. She was the first steamer to cross the Atlantic in a westerly direction.

About 1840, they attempted to run a regular steam Atlantic service, but this was a failure and it was not until 1871 that the Holland-Amerika Line was started. In the previous year the Nederland Line had established a regular service to the East Indies by way of the Suez Canal. In 1882 the Royal West India Mail Company was founded, and in 1883 the Rotterdam Lloyd emerged out of a number of smaller concerns controlled by Ruys and Son.

Other companies followed and won an excellent reputation for the cleanliness and regularity of their passenger ships and for the efficiency of their cargo side. The result was a

ROTTERDAMSCHE LLOYD
KONINKLIJKE NEDERLANDSCHE POSTVAART.

WEKELIJKSCHE AFVAARTEN VAN ROTTERDAM NAAR NEDERL. INDIE EN TERUG
HOOFDAGENTEN. RUYS & Cº., ROTTERDAM
JAVA AGENTEN: INTERNATIONALE CREDIET- EN HANDELSVEREENIGING "ROTTERDAM" BATAVIA

TROPICAL HOLLAND
THE ARCHIPELAGO OF ETERNAL SUMMER

Above and below.
Under the Dutch Flag: on the exotic Eastern route of a typical grey-hulled Dutch liner, the *dramatis personae* included tea and rubber planters, colonial high commissioners, spice merchants, missionaries, nurses, scientists and civil servants.

great increase in their business, although they always kept the economic purpose of their ships in mind and seldom built to any extreme size or speed.

During the war of 1914-18 the neutral position of Holland was frequently one of great difficulty and individual loss, but financially the Dutch shipping industry made enormous profits at this time. These were, as a general rule, wisely conserved for the slump which practical Dutch minds realized must inevitably follow the boom.

On the other hand, the Allies demanded the use of a number of Dutch ships for war purposes in return for bunker coal. The Germans sank these ships with their submarines just as they did those of any other country, although Germany was largely dependent on Holland for such contraband as contrived to slip through the British blockade.

A good deal of tonnage had to be requisitioned by the Dutch Government to maintain the country's grain supplies, and many of the passenger services had to be suspended owing to the risk to life. In spite of it all, Dutch shipping prospered as it never had before, and a considerable proportion of the excess profit earned was carefully laid aside to build new ships as soon as the opportunity arose. On the North Atlantic the Holland-Amerika Line is the principal company, its finest ship being the *Statendam,* of 28,291 tons gross. She was built in 1929 to replace a ship of the same name commandeered by the British Government while under construction at Belfast and later sunk by a German submarine.

On the South American trade the Royal Holland Lloyd was the principal company and formerly had a big passenger fleet. Between Holland and the Dutch East Indies the big

The colloquial "P. & O.", regarded as the "Cunard of the East", was pre-eminent in the trade to India and Australia at the highpoint of the British Empire. In the pioneer years of European trade with China, the pirate always had to be reckoned with and early steamers of the Line put to sea fully armed.

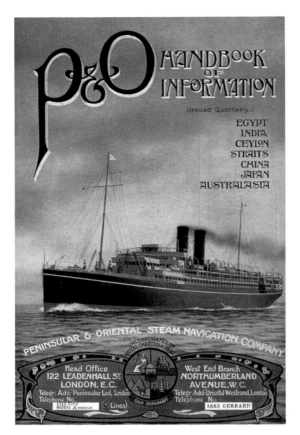

trade is virtually monopolized by the two biggest companies under the Dutch flag, the Rotterdam Lloyd and the Nederland Line. They maintain regular services with exceptionally comfortable passenger liners and some of the finest cargo motor-ships afloat.

The crack passenger ships of the Rotterdam Lloyd are the *Baloeran* and the *Dempo.* The Nederland Line also maintains magnificent motor-driven passenger ships; the Koninklijke Paketvaart Company is more interested in the secondary services in the East Indies. The Java-China-Japan Line, the United Netherlands Company, including the Holland Australia Line, the Holland West Africa Line and others maintain the services that their names suggest.

Popular Miniature Liners

The Dutch have also shown extraordinary ability and efficiency on the short sea trades, along the coasts of the Continent and also across the North Sea to and from England. The mail service between Rotterdam and London, maintained by the little miniature liners of the Batavier Line and the allied Zeeland Company's packet service between Harwich and Flushing are exceedingly popular with passengers.

THE NIEUW AMSTERDAM
The Studio, 1938

The *Nieuw Amsterdam,* the largest ship ever built in Holland and the latest comer in the Trans-Atlantic service, is distinguished both in its architecture and its decoration. It is a superb looking ship, boasting pleasant proportions and a graceful modern profile. It is superb also in its interior fitment which has been designed by Holland's greatest architects, designers and craftsmen. One is reminded that the Dutch are eminently a people of the sea – that, in the bargain, they have a wonderful tradition of art, of whose vitality to-day the *Nieuw Amsterdam* is a proof.

In comparison with the other new ocean giants of the world, it does not profess to be the largest or the fastest, but in the quality of its decoration it can rightly claim a superlative.

It is without doubt a comfortable ship – the completeness of its air conditioning and the luxury of its bathroom equipment are examples: but it has more than comfort. It is based on practical and rational planning but it has more than that. It is definitely not a collection of skittishly exuberant and fancy decoration. It has the outstanding advantage of a controlled scheme which combines architecture and decoration together in beautiful unity.

Together with sixteen architects, the painters, the sculptors, the glass workers, and fine craftsmen of the Netherlands have collaborated with understanding. The result is not merely decoration applied – it is decoration that springs from the very nature of the architectural treatment. To all those interested in art – and art in its widest sense ranging from the skilful fashioning of a useful thing to the bold handling of an imaginative theme, the *Nieuw Amsterdam* has fresh inspiration to offer, the inspiration of a positive and harmonious achievement.

100

The Grand Hall, in this respect, is one of the ship's triumphs. It was designed by Hendrik T. Wijdeweld, one of those forward looking architects who combine the enthusiasm of the dreamer with the ability of the practical man. In symphonic grey and silver it provides a background of subtle variations, designed to act as a foil to the gay colours of women's dresses and the moving panorama of life on board. When full, it becomes a lively and continually changing composition of colour. John Raedecker was responsible for the main decoration in natural coloured aluminium. Of Raedecker it has been said that nothing finer and loftier has probably been done in the whole realm of contemporary Dutch art than his monument at Wassenaar, inspired by the famous lines from *The Tempest* – "we are such stuff as dreams are made on." His ceiling, representing the course of human life, amply maintains his great reputation. In relation to its rhythmic movement and to the subdued colour scheme the murals executed by Gerard V.A. Roling, and conveying a symbolic idea – the principles of harmony and disharmony – play their part well.

There are several such focusing points. Everyone must pause before the very beautiful bronze panel of *The Four Seasons* by Jan Eloy and Leo Brom in the Cabin Class Reception Vestibule, the figures being of a rich golden hue on an emerald green background. The brothers Brom are representatives of that astonishingly vigorous school of modern sculptors in Holland. Another point of focus is the boldly carved sculpture by Fritz van Hall on the stairs to the Ritz Carlton Room, which has real grandeur of design.

The Third Class Smoking Room, designed by Frits Spanjaard, presents the latest experiment in wall decoration – the photographic mural, and there is no doubt that the excellent photographs by Eva Fernhout-Besnyo, of the cheese market, tulip fields, ships by the quay side and other aspects of Dutch life, play a very decorative part in the appearance of the room.

Taken in all the ship is extremely rich in the quantity and quality of craftsmanship. Stained glass, engraved glass, painting, lacquer work,

inlaid wood, tapestry, rugs, table tops, are all the vehicles of modern design. The glass panels by Joep Nicolas in the Cabin Class Dining Room deserve particular attention. They are carried out in *vermurail* work, the invention of the artist. The various effects are secured by a secret annealing process, after the designs have been traced with metal oxides. They have a dusky glow and depict pastoral scenes in compositions that are always interesting. Seven years ago Aldous Huxley wrote of Joep Nicolas's stained glass, "Only those who have seen Mr. Nicolas's windows in the rooms for which they were designed can realise what an important part stained glass might play in the modern decorative scheme". The celebrated novelist had earlier remarked that modern stained glass seemed wrong but that he had been won over to it by Nicolas's work at the Paris *Sallon des Decorateurs*. The panels are a further proof of the possibilities of stained glass and the gifts of this artist.

Andreas D. Copier is also responsible for some excellent glass work. Copier is head designer to the Leerdam Glass Factory whose products rank with the Swedish glass in contemporary repute. An outstanding example

Statendam III, pictured in a lithographic poster by Cassandre. Flagship of the Holland-America Line, her arrival in New York on her maiden voyage coincided with the three-hundredth anniversary of the arrival of the first Dutch ship in America (*D'Halve Maen*). Holland-America Line cruised extensively to the West Indies, South America and Bermuda, routes on which the *Statendam* proved most economical for a liner of her size.

of his work is the lift shaft with deep-sea motifs, a collaboration with Jaap Gidding. Gidding is responsible for four large decorative fish panels in the Tourist Class Dining Room, carried out with synthetic transparent lacquer on wood – another instance of the Dutch designers' deep interest in the novel use of modern materials. Of many other decorative features, whose number is so many that one cannot hope to enumerate them all here, mention may be made of the unusual rug designs – Hildegard Brom-Fischer's hand woven carpet with the signs of the Zodiac and J. J. P. Oud and Han Polak's lounge carpet with a jovial pattern of Dutch and American scenes and objects, windmills and skyscrapers, etc.

The range of artistic effort extends from one end of the ship to the other, and it is by no means confined to the public rooms, but also to the cabins and the smallest details of their equipment. The choice of woods, the harmony of light tones, the pleasant texture of fabrics, have been thought out with the same care as the wall paintings and the carvings. In the

luxurious private bathrooms with which he is provided, the cabin passenger may, for instance, observe that the water jug has very delightful proportions and that its shape is well adapted to its purpose. He may notice also that the numerals on his cabin door have an agreeable simplicity, or that the panel by his bed has a satisfying architectural relation to the wall in which it is placed. In a cabin de luxe designed by Wouda, one of the Dutch artists who have had great influence on the trend of modern decoration, one has that sense of a restrained, but very liveable scheme which is the ideal of to-day. The same good taste is evident in Tourist and Third Class Cabins.

In the combination of rational comfort with all the arts that minister to the pleasures of seeing, the *Nieuw Amsterdam* is certainly a big achievement. In 1609 Henry Hudson reported to his principals, the Netherlands East India Company in Amsterdam, that the island of Manhattan was "a very pleasant place to build a town on". One can report to-day that the *Nieuw Amsterdam* is a very pleasant ship to send to the great city which has come out of the original Nieuw Amsterdam.

Travellers from the New World especially will find in it a culture linked with their own in its modernity, but distinct in itself and characteristic of the finer side of the European mind, still rich in creative thought and energy.

THE MODERN SHIP'S WIRELESS
P. R. Bird

At twenty minutes to six on a dark January morning in the North Atlantic, the look-out in the liner *Republic* saw a large vessel loom without warning from the surrounding fog, crash into the *Republic* on the port side and sheer away. With a suddenly flooded engine-room and an alarming list, the *Republic* floundered alone in the fog with 710 souls on board – and the ship's wireless set. In this setting the wireless installation was called upon to prove its value. There followed a demonstration which thrilled the world, and led to a universal demand that all large ships should be fitted with wireless apparatus.

Marconi took out the first patent for wireless telegraphy in 1896. Its value as a means of saving life was proved in its earliest days and by 1919 the Marconi Company had designed apparatus for use in lifeboats. On larger liners ship-to-shore telegraphy was installed for passengers wanting to telephone to the shore.

The collision occurred on January 23, 1909, in latitude 40° 17' N., longitude 70° W. The *Republic,* bound for Madeira, had left New York the day before, and during the night had run into a belt of fog. The vessel was proceeding slowly about twenty-six miles south of Nantucket Light, when she was rammed by the Italian steamer *Florida.*

Only six lives were lost when the vessels crashed together, but about 2,000 people were placed in imminent danger, for both ships were seriously damaged in the collision. The *Florida,* groping her way back and guided by fog signals, first took on board all the passengers. The doomed *Republic* sank, but not before her wireless had summoned the *Baltic* and other vessels. They reached the scene in time, transferred passengers and crews, and landed all those involved in the collision without further loss of life.

The quality of the seamanship displayed on that occasion, the swift transfer in boats, the rescue of the *Republic's* captain and crew when the vessel sank – these were all in the tradition of the sea. Further, a new tradition was inaugurated in the far-flung distress message, summoning vessels many miles out of sight by electromagnetic waves. On that occasion wireless, the new invention, vindicated itself as a large-scale life saver; apparatus similar to that of the *Republic* was soon fitted to other ships, and within a few years it was proved beyond question in all kinds of emergencies that science had provided mankind with another powerful aid to preserve the safety of life at sea.

The modern liner's radio apparatus is, of course, entirely different from those early wireless installations. It is at once more powerful and more sensitive – literally millions of times more sensitive. The original ships' wireless sets were designed primarily for safety: that they adequately served their purpose is recorded in many a story of rescued lives. In the modern liner the safety of life is still the primary purpose of the radio equipment. International laws compel all shipowners to fit certain classes of vessel with wireless transmitters and receivers, and to arrange that wireless watch shall be kept, in conformity with the various International Conventions for the Safety of Life at Sea. The means, however, have outstripped the end in view; and instead of being merely the instrument of making distress calls when tragedy has occurred, wireless is now devoted more to prevention than to cure.

To-day the liner bound across the Atlantic can communicate with radio stations in Canada and the U.S.A. before she has left Southampton Water, and she can easily exchange messages with sister ships plying anywhere on the route. She receives and sends out weather reports. She checks her chronometers by the time signals coming direct from observatory clocks. She has on board a wireless direction-finder that is absolutely independent of fog or any similar condition of bad visibility. Furthermore, not only is the captain kept in touch with his owners and with other vessels, but passengers are also continuously linked with friends at home and with business acquaintances by wireless. Most of the communications from ship to ship, or between ship and shore, are telegraphed in the Morse code, because this method is superior for fast long-distance working. But the larger vessels are equipped also with telephonic apparatus. The telephone in the ship then enables a passenger to take a call which has come through from a telephone subscriber ashore and to answer as though from house to house. Since about ninety-five per cent of the world's telephones are now interconnected by wireless and cables, there is scarcely a place in the world that cannot be communicated with by telephone from a liner in mid-ocean.

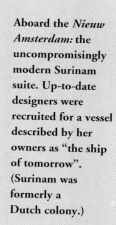

Wireless-Equipped Lifeboats

In some of the larger ships a passenger may speak from any of the ship's telephones in the public rooms, or from his private cabin. Connection is made between the wireless room and the selected telephone through the liner's switchboard; thus the call between ship and shore can be made as conveniently as from one house to another in the same town.

There are also several other valuable applications of wireless technique that assist the seafarer. The Merchant Shipping Act now provides that all passenger-carrying vessels of 5,000 tons gross and upwards shall be fitted with wireless direction-finding apparatus. The invention of this equipment solved, once and for all, the navigator's age-old problem of finding the ship's position in fog or haze, which hides the sun, stars and horizon and thus prevents the use of the sextant.

Lifeboat sets are another part of the large liner's wireless equipment. In the event of the boat becoming separated from others its miniature wireless set is able to serve the small community in much the same way as the main installation serves the ship herself. Electric waves are used also for depth-sounding, the method depending upon a train of waves being directed down to the bed of the ocean. The waves are reflected back to the ship and indicate the depth below by means of the time they take in transit. The apparatus can be worked from a single accumulator, and is hundreds of times faster in operation than the best wire-sounding machine. The downward-directed waves used in this method are more of the nature of sound than of wireless waves, but their detection and amplification on return from the ocean bed are an electrical process for which valve amplifiers are used.

Wireless apparatus in a ship includes the loudspeaker and amplifier equipment for distributing speech and music throughout the vessel. Apparatus of this kind is able to reproduce vocal music, the ship's orchestra, gramophone records or speech; and it may be used in conjunction with a broadcast receiver for supplying programmes from shore stations to the various loudspeakers in the equipment.

These subsidiary applications of wireless are, however, of minor importance compared with the main transmitter and receiver, on which the ship depends for reliable communications.

Aboard the *Nieuw Amsterdam:* the uncompromisingly modern Surinam suite. Up-to-date designers were recruited for a vessel described by her owners as "the ship of tomorrow". (Surinam was formerly a Dutch colony.)

"Morning Bathe" on the *Strathmore*, circa 1937, by Agnes B. Warburg. Warburg's photograph shows the open bathing pool on C deck. The luxurious *Strathmore*, built and engined by Vickers-Armstrong, captured the Blue Riband of the passage from Mediterranean ports to India on her maiden voyage.

Away From It All

"One travels without constant packing and unpacking, noise or dust. And one travels in one's hotel"

The Queen magazine

ARE YOU ABOARD?
K.K. Bowker
Harper's Bazaar, 1934

When you simply can't face yourself in the mirror a-mornings; when you feel like a piece of toast on which a poached egg has lingered and grown cold; when you lie in bed wishing you were a heart-breaking beauty or Sir James Jeans, that you could play the xylophone with your teeth or had a passion for green ivories – then there is just one thing can save you. Clutch at the telephone with your clammy hand. Order yourself a dozen new countries on appro ... a new face, a new feeling ! You'll get the first part of the pick-me-up in a fat packet next morning ... It's a cruise !

When you feel your toes tingling, and pirouette at the sight of a policeman; when you have no craving to be Noel Coward, and could say good morning to a mule; when you feel an overdraft would be an asset and six new hats are an instant necessity; when you want to buzz across the housetops and flip the Man-in-the-Moon beneath the chin – Why ! walk the plank my hearties ... walk the long, long gang plank ... It's a cruise !

High above the docks the tall ship towers, white as Humpty-Dumpty on his great wall. Triple-belted with decks. Each studded with small button-faces. Unknown as yet, some of them will be sewn into your life...Canvas-covered tubes tie the ship to the pierhead. Now you are a link in the long chain of people pouring through. Ship's officers snap through passports, pause at yours. For one shuddering moment you feel yourself a Latroslavruskian spy. But no ! The photographer's dark ruse has failed. Your true self is recognised with a quick smile, and you move on.

Inside, it's a hurricane pudding, undergoing a seaworthy stir. Pick out your plums ! Fat women in sables, slim girls in roughish uffish coats, soigne charmers in mink; orchids, roses, spicy carnations a-bloom in every collar. Plump men baying about in flannels ... tall men with lean faces. Flower-boxes as long as Cupid's arrows hurtling on their way to cabins ... imperturbable smiling men in blue, with

peaked caps ... stewardesses, blue and white like Scyllas and Charybdises in neat rows against the wall. Stewards, boys, telegrams, letters, last-minute friends ....

"ALL VISITORS ASHORE !"

Dash to the side. Snatch a place near the rail. Someone waves across your shoulder. Bumps your bouquet. Apologises. Your eyes meet in the expectant appraisal that may mean – anything – for the future. The ship's away !

The cabin is gay with glass and polished panelling – lights galore. Piled to the portholes with luggage. Boxes and baskets. Flowers, sweets, smokes fruit, more mail, air-mail, radiograms. A steadying stream of stewards stewardesses, deck boys. Now for the ship's officers. Every ship publishes a brochure "How to distinguish the Captain from the Cabin-boy". Stripes, dots, squares, bands, circles. But it is impossible to carry list-in-head about ship, impossible to carry list-in-hand for ready application. Here are some unmistakable signs. The captain is usually recognised in the dining-room by his empty place; on the bridge-deck by a sibilant hiss which says "No miss, not now – captain's sleeping", face to face by affability and

charm, and the peak of his cap. All other ranks are peaked and plain. Captain shelters his eyes with a mass of gold oak-leaves (on English liners). Maple leaves, on C.P.R. liners.

The staff captain is a bowdlerised version of the above. The purser is instantly recognisable as the worst-badgered and best-tempered man on the ship. Listens with rapt sympathy to all enquiries and/or complaints fair and/or foolish. Promises results to 80 per cent. Achieves them to 91 per cent. Has a wiling, beguiling eye, that invariably comes to rest on adored wife and seven children, safeguardingly ashore. Is the master of the best cocktails ever shaken on the ship, and can toss a party like a pancake.

Engineers, chief and second go cannily in black uniforms. Delightful but difficult. If not Scotch, should be. The doctor is known by the thin red line that runs among the gold. Out rather for *berlud* than for money. Mostly musical tastes.

Chief and second stewards have wavy gold lines on cuffs, instantly suggesting drinks. Deck stewards are acrobats complete with trays. Easily distinguished, and often obtainable. The chef is known (and worth

knowing) by the full-rigged mainsail above his brow. Refuse to tour his kingdom in group formation. Make a personal point of contact – and the world is yours !

The ship's company knows no age limit in any class. *Cruisers* may be plump or stringy. They are well-travelled, pleasant mannered, available when wanted, but curiously protective in colouring. Draw, but never demand, friendship. Weathered but not withered. *Cruiseens* are gay lads with a spark of adventure in their bright, clear eyes. Ozone-minded. Active, alert. Soften under the influence of beauty, moonlight, music and mixed drinks. *Cruisettes* are mermaids who tell no tales. The dearest, dashingest darlings who ever cut a heart or scuttled round a ship. Provocative. Inventive. Joyous. Expensive, but immune from all the chills of life. *Cruiseringoes* are a separate class. Under this heading lump: those who are physically chained to smoke-room and bar throughout the cruise. One or two more who should be, for protection of passengers. (Type almost extinct.) Everyone YOU don't like. And possibly those lost souls who always appear for the first time forty-eight hours before you reach the final debarking port.

And now for ten, twenty, or one hundred days of dalliance. Punctuated by a peerless cuisine. Gayest of games. Movies, concerts, lectures cards, the daily pools on the ship's run. The salt pool where there's sloshing and splashing. You can plunge in either ! The children's supervised paradise. The electric menagerie in the gymnasium. Horse racing on deck, shuffle-board, quoits, tennis: a treasure hunt where queer clues send you careering. "Funsports" with their uproarious jollity. Daily dancing – gala night, with gaiety more catching than a cold – feathery fantastics, and flying fancies, and all the balloons in the world going up!

Intervening ports of call are slices of life, handed on a plate like cake: light, rich, indigestible, scrunchy. Northern lights, or tom-toms beating in the dark mysterious forests. Crisp breezes, and the languor of the tropics. A fairy story – a romance – a play. With yourself in the principal part. A life that never was on land, and only comes at sea. It's a cruise !

109

A Bridge Party: a cruise was one long party, with the added attraction of visits to foreign ports and sunny excursions in the hinterland. Many mothers took their daughters on cruises in the hope of finding them husbands and shipping companies advertised their success as "Cupid's agents".

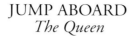

The Booth Line provided cruises to the Amazon, one of the most unusual of the longer cruises, travelling 1,000 miles up river to the city of Manaos, passing Para, a city where East and West were found side by side. According to *The Queen* magazine (1936), "one can almost throw a ship's biscuit into the trees on either hand".

JUMP ABOARD
The Queen

Cruising isn't what it used to be. Once the pastime of the very idle and the very rich, it is now within reach of everyone. There are all sorts of tours and all sorts of accommodations which will fit any sized purse, but they all have one thing in common. Whatever you spend you get just about the best possible value for your money. Whether you jump aboard a United States liner for a twenty- or twenty-one day trip that gives you six or seven days in New York (and for how little !), or spend two weeks in the Mediterranean in a P. and O. liner, or join the Canadian Pacific liner *Empress of Australia* for the Seven Seas Cruise in February, or go round the world in the *Franconia,* you may be sure that you will be living life in the way to which you are accustomed if you are blessed with healthy finances, and in the way to which you would like to become accustomed if you aren't !

KOTOR DALMATIA–ATMOSPHERE: Pines, cliffs, ramparts, and brigands – the latter picturesque and polite. **TO DO:** Motor anywhere. Dubrovnik, mediaeval and full of charm. Montenegro with her lunar rocks, farther still Albania, a paintbox of local colour. **TO EAT**: Fish, flesh and fowl all spendidly spiced. Pasta, lobster with saffron rice. **DON'T MISS:** The petticoated chieftains, the trousered Moslem beauties. The Dalmatian coast. It's unlike anything except itself. **WARNING:** The language can only be described as a bad habit. Some travellers have imagined it a fit.

PHOTOGRAPHY
The Queen, 1903

The most satisfactory way of taking either ships or yachts is three-quarters on. If attempted broadside-on, when in motion, the result will probably be blurred, unless a focal plane shutter working at high speed is employed. Taken directly end on, the effect in most cases is decidedly inartistic. In the first instance, the life, dash, and movement of the waves can be captured, and a capital picture is generally secured. There is always a certain degree of uncertainty when using an ordinary hand camera, lest the whole object should not be on the plate. A picture shorn of its upperhalf is not at all satisfactory. The best plan is to use rather a small stop watch till the object appears fairly large in the finder, and then give a quick exposure. Absolutely the best camera for shipping work is a twin lens; next to that comes one of the single lens "Reflex" type, such as are made by Shew, Adams, and the Primus Camera Company. The advantage of seeing what is on the plate at the moment of exposure cannot be overrated.

IN DEFENCE OF PLEASURE CRUSING
Harper's Bazaar, 1930

An Apologia For The New Kind Of Vagabondage

by Evelyn Waugh

It was with thoroughly mixed feelings, as they say, that I climbed the big bastion overlooking the harbour at Malta, and caught my first glimpse of the *Stella Polaris.* I had arranged to go for a cruise in her and felt shy about it, for the whole idea did violence to a great many preconceived prejudices.

Every Englishman abroad assumes himself to be a traveller and despises his fellow-countrymen as tourists. As far as I can discover this is a distinction which disturbs no race but

112

quite enterprising and distinguished to have been abroad at all. The typical traveller then was the young man fresh from the University, preparing for a political career; he went on a tour of the Courts of Europe, furnished with coach and courier and letters of introduction; he admired the Italian marbles, commented on the beauty of Spanish ladies and the agricultural methods of the peasant proprietors; perhaps he even fought a duel.

Trains, guide-books and travel agencies soon took most of the grandeur from the Grand Tour. In the second Empire the Englishman abroad is represented by the "Paterfamilias" of Punch, ignorant of the language, impatient of the institutions and suspicious of the food of the countries he visits. By his side goes the Travelling Spinster, adept in the brewing of tea in hotel bedrooms: she attributes faulty-sanitation to the terrible errors of the Romish faith and is very careful about locking her door at night. Finally, at the end of the century came the massed attack of the lower middle class having its annual jaunt. This evil is still with us and needs no description.

In his *Path to Rome* Mr. Belloc invented a new ideal traveller – a cheerful and dishevelled pilgrim, trudging from inn to inn with a piece

our own; with us it is the cause of much genuine pride and humiliation. Up to that morning in Malta, however abject my dependence on dragomen or travel agencies, I, too, had been a slave to this particular *snobbisme;* but it was clear to me that the moment I went on board the *Stella* I should have crossed that very imaginary line. I should no longer be able to look up from my café table with wonder and contempt as fleets of cars bore their "personally conducted" parties on the quest of culture. There could be no more hair splitting – I was frankly and wholly a tourist.

I do not know who started the *snobbisme* about uncomfortable travelling, but I think that Mr. Hilaire Belloc's *Path to Rome* is very largely responsible. Clearly, at the beginning of this century, some change of attitude was necessary. There were three successive types of English traveller in the nineteenth century. In the days before mechanical transport it was

MONTEVIDEO – ATMOSPHERE: Karl Marx surrounded by Moab. Very modern and experimental, except in February carnival, when everyone goes gay. Average age then 7 years. **TO DO:** drive out to Carrasco, the Monte Carlo of the South. Twenty miles of beach. Ride over the horizon. Gamble at the Casino. Dance on a marble terrace. **TO EAT:** An outsize in prawns. Langoustes and Canellonis, which are stuffed pancakes. Also native dishes – asado and puchero. **DON'T MISS:** Lunching at Cavellini's – a log-hut under the pines at Carrasco. **WARNING:** When the North wind blows it's like an oven. Nobody keeps their heads, hats or engagements.

Cruises ran to Norway, Spain and Portugal, Morocco, the Canaries, and the western Mediterranean. In the thirties, advertised cruises suited middle-class people who could not afford Continental holidays because of a depreciation of sterling, but who wanted a change from the English seaside.

113

of garlic sausage in his pocket and a huge bottle of wine on his shoulders, singing and chatting and breathing in the spirit of the country. All the world was his garden, said Mr. Belloc, since men made railways and gave him leave to keep away from them. Well that was all very nice and jolly, but since then men have made motorcars and aeroplanes and there is no keeping away from *them*. So that ideal has had to pass, too, and its place has been taken by another kind of vagabondage which is held up to us by nearly all the young men and women who get publishers to pay them to leave the country.

The modern ideal traveller is laudably vague about his plans; he is also, publishers being what they are, usually rather short of money; his two chief delights are bed-bugs and consuls who refuse to cash cheques; he has fun in low night clubs, he visits several exalted houses, and generally discovers a neglected masterpiece or two. If he is lucky he hits upon some whole period of art that has been neglected (he hurries back to his publisher and tries to get a commission to write about it; the publisher points out fourteen or fifteen standard works on the subject, and there the matter ends). I have done a certain amount of this kind of travelling and it is great fun. And it is no good trying to expect that sort of fun on a pleasure cruise. However, there are compensations.

For one thing there is luggage. I defy anyone in the world to derive any amusement from coping with luggage day after day at docks and railway stations and frontiers, from unpacking and repacking a mysteriously increasing collection of books and drawing materials and photographs and dirty clothes and antiques. For the ten days before the arrival of the *Stella*, I had not spent more than two consecutive nights in the same hotel or ship or train. The satisfaction of unpacking my trunk once and for all and pushing it under the bed, of arranging ties and shirts and handkerchiefs in a chest of drawers, hanging up my suits in a wardrobe, filling a large laundry bag and knowing that I was settled there for a month, made up for the romance

WHITBREAD'S PALE ALE

of a great deal of promiscuous adventure. Then there are passports. It may be something to talk about afterwards, but it is very dreary at the time to stand about in a draughty shed while some unshaven Balkan peasant dressed like a caricature of "little Willie" holds one's passport upside down and breathes garlic over it while he catechises one in unintelligible French about the dates of one's grandparents' marriages. It is disagreeable to be woken in the middle of the night and prodded under the arms by a half-sober doctor examining one for bubonic plague. It is boring to learn that a consulate in London has sold one a bogus visa, or to be told that the photograph in one's passport bears so close a resemblance to a murderer wanted by the New York police that one must either pay a large tip or be sent under escort to the capital. On a pleasure cruise one simply hands in one's papers to the

purser and he does all the necessary bribery.

Then there is the question of physical comfort. Nothing can be dirtier and more uncomfortable than a really bad ship (I have travelled second class on a Greek coastal steamer) and nothing can be more luxurious than a really good one. The *Stella* came from Norway and brought with her an almost glacial cleanliness; she also brought a cold buffet of Baltic delicacies which is the best I have ever encountered. I imagine the *hors d'oeuvre* of pre-war Russia to have been rather like that. There are very few hotels and certainly no trains, however expensive, which can offer the same standard of service as one meets in a ship. Hotel servants are debauched by the continual flow of one-night visitors. Ship stewards know that they have you for a long time and that there is a large tip waiting for them at the end of the cruise if they take trouble. And they do take trouble. I think the deck steward on the *Stella* (oh! those pert Alf's and Dan's and Sid's of fashionable urban cocktail bars !) fulfilled almost completely the Jeeves standard of a perfect servant. I have never yet found a train on which the washing and sanitary accommodation is even adequate; in a ship it is almost invariably admirable. All these considerations are not only negligible but actively contemptible to the real travel-snob. However ....

With regard to expense, I don't think that there is much in it either way. It is definitely not a cheap form of holiday and if one's aim is simply to "get abroad" for a month it is of course, infinitely more economical to go to one place and book *pension* terms at an hotel and stay there. But if one wants to move about, unless one is a very astute traveller indeed, one soon spends as much as one does on a cruising ship for a very much lower standard of comfort. The prices of the tickets, as one looks through the gay catalogues of the shipping companies, seem immense, but one has the satisfaction of knowing that once that is over almost everything is paid for, and one is free from the continual financial jolts and jars that beset the independent traveller. Besides, in a

115

ship there is none of that organised avarice that the tourist finds on land. The head office have collected your money and the aim of everyone on board is simply to make you comfortable. Another consideration which weighs a great deal more heavily with some people than others is that one can buy tobacco and spirits duty free as soon as one leaves port.

But the greatest joy is one's fellow passengers. Here I think a ship of the *Stella's* size – she is a 6,000 ton motor-yacht carrying rather under two hundred passengers – has an advantage over the big liners. In a month's time one gets to know a great deal about almost everyone. It is like a vast house party without any kind of mutual obligations. At hotels one falls into unplumbed depths of speculation about the people at the next table and then they suddenly disappear and one is left in an abyss of unsatisfied curiosity. In a ship one has prolonged proximity. There are twenty novels implicit in every cruise. The main bulk of the passengers are elderly couples of comfortable means, with or without daughters, who are avoiding the English winter. These are often most agreeable companions but they are the least interesting – at any rate to a professional novelist. But even they often reveal unsuspected depths; it is extraordinary to see how people change and expand in sea air. The daughters, too, almost invariably fall in love. There is inevitably a great deal of falling in love on board ship and inevitably, too, it has to happen more or less in the open. The boat deck during dances is a great centre of romance.

There is usually at least one honeymoon couple on any cruise. It is very odd that there should be. I can imagine no *milieu* in which I would less readily spend a honeymoon. However, there it is. Another very interesting type which swarms to sea is the widow of early middle age. These are women who have spent the first half of their lives dutifully managing a home and children; they find themselves rather embarrassed by their sudden independence; their children are safely stowed away at boarding schools and they set out to "see the world". The most illuminating thing about

them is the things they buy. I suppose it is the shopping habit, engrained into them from over-much housekeeping, suddenly run riot. They buy almost anything. Every port has its special line of tourist's trophy; tortoiseshell combs and lava animals at Naples, shawls at Venice, olive wood toys at Corfu, lace at Malta, brass horrors everywhere in North Africa, beads, inlaid gun metal and very shocking picture postcards at Port Said, bogus antiquities at Piraeus, live tortoises in Crete. At Cana in Galilee I was offered one of the original wine jars in which the miracle was performed for a little less than five shillings; at Constantinople a curious trade is done in English silver coinage, there is horrible arts-and-crafts basket work at Majorca and things are offered for sale in Algiers which it is not seemly to mention. And at every port the widows buy everything that is offered to them. I wonder what becomes of them afterwards. Have they innumerable relatives who expect presents or are there, all over the country, houses filled with the spoils of these cruises ? Or do they just crumble away and vanish like the beastly souvenirs they give one in night clubs on "gala" nights ? Or are they perhaps sent to the hospitals ? One cannot doubt however that they have served their purpose when one sees the happy collectors comparing their day's marketing after dinner. I suppose it is a blissful change after biscuits and electric light bulbs and children's winter underclothes.

Another fascinating class are the organisers. They "get up" hymn singing on Sunday evenings, and concerts and fancy dress balls and bridge tournaments, and throw themselves into the deck sports with unaffected enthusiasm. I heard two "organisers" discussing a fellow-passenger. "I don't think," said one of them "that he's really pulling his weight in this ship".

There is a much less agreeable sort of "organiser" that occasionally turns up, who spends his time agitating for letters of protest to the captain or the shipping company about some fancied impropriety or defect.

There are usually some admirable examples of social climbers and also of social outsiders. It is fun when these two find themselves playing

STAMBOUL – ATMOSPHERE: "Bubbles blown of dreams" – domes and minarets reflected in the Golden Horn. **TO DO:** See the Mosques and palaces. Sail, or be rowed in a *caique.* Spend hours in the labyrinthine markets. Go to Angora for a sight of modern Turkey, to a cemetery on Fridya for a glimpse of the old. **TO EAT:** Loucoums and Turkish delight. French cooking at the big hotels. Sticky local delicacies such as mincemeat and rice rolled in vine leaves at the *suq* restautants. Drink araki if your head will stand it. **DON'T MISS:** Sunset across the Golden Horn. The imperial collection of soapstone. **WARNING:** The streets are cobbled. In Pera they are also extremely steep.

together in the deck games. There is also the type of snob who shuns his fellow passengers and is only happy discussing navigation with the officers. He is rather ostentatiously unsympathetic in rough weather.

There are innumerable other types and individuals – for instance, the sham *grande dame* who has all her meals sent to her cabin because she was not invited to the captain's table – and there can be no better opportunity than a ship for detailed observation. The time when one is inclined to find them boring is when one meets them on shore. One imagines that one has discovered a restaurant and in come six familiar faces; one is just getting rather elated by some piece of architecture when twenty-five of them arrive complete with a guide. One meets them most embarrassingly when one is sampling low life. This is the fear that most intellectual people have of pleasure cruising: the dislike of going about everywhere in a crowd. Well, that is a thing one has to make up one's mind to.

Often it doesn't matter at all. At some obviously show place such as Pompeii or the Serai at Constantinople, one's companions can do nothing to hinder one's appreciation, and can add a great deal to one's amusement by their comments. At places like Ragusa or Catarro one is clearly at a disadvantage. But

that is because one has a preconceived idea of what travelling ought to be like. One must make up one's mind that cruising is a pursuit entirely of its own kind. It is not a bogus kind of travelling, but an entirely new sport, with its own aims and rules. One sets out primarily for rest and change of scene and comfort and one certainly gets that, and one's recreation should not be the study of foreign places and people but the study of one's fellow-passengers among foreign places; and to the right-minded person that should be a source of exquisite and abiding delight.

SPRING HOLIDAYS AND CRUISES
The Queen, 1936

Cruising holidays are still among the most popular of all, and to-day the facilities for taking them are amazing. Fares are low, comfort is high, and the choice of one's destination is only dependent on one's taste, the time available for the holiday, and the amount one can afford to spend upon it.

All the big steamship companies have nowadays delightful cruises to various parts of the world, and by them one can enjoy the experience of visiting strange and interesting countries, while at the same time the fatigue of travel is minimised. There are, too, the attractions of enlarging one's circle of friends and acquaintances, joining, when one cares to do so, in the bright social life of a big hotel – which is what the liners really are nowadays – and the varied recreations and sports which form an important portion of the programme.

Fortunately not only have all tastes been catered for, but there are cruises of all lengths. One need not devote six months to a cruise, even a month, for there are short cruises of a most enjoyable character from ten days upwards to a fortnight or three days in length. And in the fortnight or three weeks holiday a trip to the Mediterranean; a cruise in the Norwegian fiords; one in the Baltic; or one to the Atlantic island is possible; while, in less time than that, one can visit several Spanish and Portuguese ports and catch a glimpse of North Africa.

Seen at Monte Carlo: the *Empress of Britain*, prima donna of the Canadian Pacific Line, took King George VI to North America in 1939. Details of the Queen's wardrobe (she devoted the last three days before departure to final fittings) intrigued the American public. One New York paper was reported to be offering $1000 for sketches of her new wardrobe.

In an age without aircraft competition, cruise ships also catered for port-to-port passengers and were in receipt of mail contracts. Cargo space might include insulated chambers suitable for the carriage of fruit, meat and other perishable goods over long distances.

118

In the longer cruises, visits to the West Coast of Africa, South Africa, South America, the West Indies, India, Ceylon, the Far East, Australia, and New Zealand can be paid; while those who have five months or a little more to spare can take a trip of some 40,000 miles round and about the world.

The cruising holiday should appeal to most people because of the variety of interests afforded, and the possibilities it has for an amazing number of new experiences. There is nothing dull about it. Everything to those who have not been on a cruise is novel and even exciting, and for old stagers the cruise never loses its charm. There is just that element of leisured luxury that appeals to most people very strongly, and the whole personnel of an ocean-going cruising liner is skillfully adjusted to contribute to the comfort, happiness and enjoyment of the passengers. A landsman never knows, and can only guess, the amount of painstaking organisation which has gone to making a holiday cruise successful. But the guess will not be far short of the mark if it takes the form of the phrase, "an immensity of labour and thought".

There is certainly no form of holiday that is at one and the same time so restful in this strenuous age, and so interesting. "One travels," as one enthusiastic cruising holiday-taker puts it, "without constant packing and unpacking, noise or dust. And one travels in one's hotel."

WANTED – ON ANY VOYAGE
what travel clothes to take … and not to take
Vogue, 1939

* Go up the gang-plank in a warm coat. A great lip-stick red coat is wonderful, worn over a beige suit. A red coat – besides being pretty effective – is an unbeatable Jack-of-all-coats. It will go amiably over town suits, prints, sports clothes … even your evening clothes.

* Unless you're bound for Cannes and smart casino night-life, or embarking on a good-time cruise, you won't want cargoes of evening clothes. One formal dress and two or three interchangeable dinner outfits will see you through. A natural linen skirt and a pair of string sweaters would be perfect in Riviera night-clubs … and they pack painlessly.

* Take along, wherever you go, the knitted or jersey turbans everyone is wearing, to twine around your head and anchor with a big gold hairpin or jewelled dagger. They pack without a whimper, keep your hair unruffled, look smart anywhere.

* Consider a plaid suit. Plaid is one of the most dust-defiant, crush-defiant travellers on earth. Take a wool plaid for a cool route; a cotton plaid suit for a warmer route – whatever your means of transport.

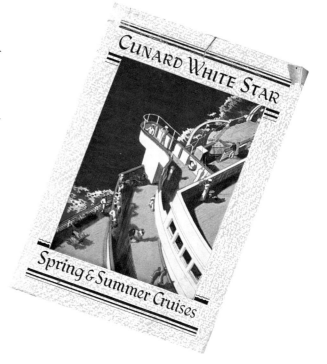

A gouache maquette for a front cover for *Harper's Bazaar*, 1937, by Cassandre. The ocean liner held a romantic appeal for artists working in both commercial and fine art.

Bright summer wear of the sort hitherto only worn by smart visitors to the South of France was popularised by cheap cruising. Girls spent most of their day in bathing-dresses or coloured linen beach-pyjamas and huge straw hats and if possible wore something excitingly different for every night of the trip.

* If you're travelling light, decide – and stick to – one basic colour scheme for all your clothes. *That* pares down to a minimum the number of accessories you have to lug along. Navy-blue, veteran travellers agree, is one of the nimblest jugglers in existence. Navy accessories would get on well with a red, navy, beige or grey top-coat or suit, your printed dresses and your sports outfit.

* Leave your finely pleated skirts at home. They need constant ironing, unless the pleats are stitched down, or are the woven-in variety.

* As a general rule, slacks don't belong on public means of transportation. On cruise ships and ocean liners, restrict them to the sun deck or swimming pool vicinity. Save your slacks for your private boats, resorts and country wear.

* If you expect to pass through several climates, you may find it simplifies matters to pack warm clothes in one bag, medium-weight clothes in another, and light-weight things in a third, and label them accordingly.

MAKE EVERY COSTUME COUNT
Vogue, 1937

A cruise wardrobe offers the greatest temptation to extravagance and fashion errors. You're in a holiday mood ... you want to look your best every minute of the time ... and you're not quite sure what you may need. So, all too often, the inexperienced "cruiser" goes up the gangplank with twice as much luggage as she should have, and still lacks the wardrobe necessities to make her trip perfect. Of course a cruise wardrobe is like any other wardrobe in one respect ... your inclinations, whether you are a sports addict, or a deck chair enthusiast, determine the character of your costumes. The length of your cruise and the type of boat also play a part. Are you ready ? Let's start to pack and dress.

"What shall I wear going aboard the boat?" You'll wear the same clothes you've been wearing for winter in town ... a *tailleur*, worn with a jersey, and over it a warm, swaggering

DOWN TO THE SEA IN SHIPS : SUMMER HOLIDAY FASHIONS.

tweed coat. Don't think you're going to sail from Southampton straight into steaming seas and sunny days. Winter is winter in England regardless of your cruise ... and it'll be days before you find midsummer weather. Will you need a coat, even then ? Indeed you will.

Now let's look over the dress scene. There are just three general types of clothes worn on a cruise – active sports clothes, spectator sports frocks, and dinner or evening dresses. Forget your afternoon frocks. But three evening frocks are not too many to take.

Each of your evening dresses should be at least two-faced. This makes for a different look each evening. One word of warning – avoid the too bulky fabrics, or the unseasonworthy sheer that droops with the first damp air. You need not stick to lace, ship valeting being what it is. But crêpe, round or flat, and easily pressed cottons are preferred. And a small electric iron is a good stowaway.

The number of spectator sports frocks you should include depends on the length of your cruise, and how active you plan to be. If you mix deck games with lounging, and are taking an average 14-day trip, you'll need at least three spectator sports frocks. Above all, don't get "fancy" or "daring" with these frocks. They

120

must be simple, workmanlike. Over one of these spectator sports frocks, you'll wear a coat when you go ashore in the various ports. So make at least one of the frocks a washable crêpe or linen in a colour to blend with that homespun coat – a natural beige frock, a brown coat; a dusty pink dress, a navy coat; a deep blue frock, a paler blue coat. For the warmest ports, you can wear your short-sleeved two piece frock, especially if you make it of a spun rayon challis or cotton suiting.

Your sports clothes should include at least one sleeveless, sun-back "tennis dress". After that requisite, the field is open. Shorts, slacks, culottes – look at your figure and make your choice. But before you rule out shorts (remembering how you looked in them two years ago), take a look at the new, longer, and kinder length. It is almost like a kiltie.

Again, assuming a two-week cruise and an average amount of games and on-looking, two sports costumes, with one extra blouse, are a minimum – and this is too little unless one of those costumes is dark and wrinkle-proof enough to stand several wearings without washing. A dark jersey or cotton lisle shirt and dark jersey or flannel slacks will give you an old reliable sports outfit that will not show wear and tear. Cotton gaberdine shorts and cotton broadcloth shirt may be light or even white – but takes two sets if you want to plan to wear them regularly. Dark, crease-resisting linen for a culotte frock and *piqu* for a sleeveless dress are sound fabric suggestions. Your bathing suit depends upon your weight, your swimming skill, and your fashion sense. That brassiere-and-bloomer set is fresh from Cannes and very chic – but stick to a dressmaker suit if your figure is no longer slim or if you have any suggestion of a "spare tyre" around your middle.

Let's sum up your suitcase now. Two or three evening dresses, each capable of variation; a warm casual coat; three spectator sports frocks; two or three active sports costumes; a bathing suit. AND one pair of rubber-soled walking shoes (comfortable but not grim), one or two pairs of evening slippers; six pairs of stockings, three pairs of anklets,

three sets of easily tubbed daytime underwear, one set of evening; a casual felt hat (a good one, please); plenty of scarves, two or three belts, two pairs of neutral tone washable gloves; a tight-topped box of clips, pins, daytime and evening adornment; a leak-proof kit of cosmetics, including a darker powder to take care of your changing skin tone. Now – visualize yourself in each costume and add the extra slip, the foundation garments, and such, that only you can prescribe. Ready ? Pack !

No passenger liner was complete wihout a games deck and a swimming pool. Outdoor pools were coming into their own by the thirties, a period which saw the Italians experimenting with real sand on lido decks.

One of the requirements of social life was the "right" clothes, for men no less than women. For both sexes, probably the most essential outdoor garment of all was the hat.

121

THE INTERIOR DESIGN OF PASSENGER SHIPS
Royal Society of Arts Journal, 1966

My grandfather, a shipowner, kept a diary during an Atlantic voyage in 1886. He was particularly interested in the means of dividing up the various classes on board, a problem which remains to this day, though there is now less social difference between classes. I believe the separation of the classes on board ship has been clung on to for too long and that the future lies in accommodating a much wider range of income groups within one class, sharing public facilities but enjoying a wide choice of cabin accommodation and perhaps, too, of eating opportunities. My grandfather noted in his diary that the inferior class out on their deck would keep peering through the skylights at the superior class in their saloon below. He made a note that in future the inside of our own ships' skylights must have ground glass panels and be made good to look at. It was clear to him that, for reasons such as he had just noted, they must often be kept shut. This brought him to the question of ventilation. In his day it was seldom possible in winter to have the portholes open. For social reasons skylights were often shut too. One attractive source of ventilation for the inside of the ship was the companionway, and this he strongly favoured. He noted that for this purpose they should always pass through the public rooms. There were two other recognized ways of ventilating, either by large openings in the floors of public rooms, to ventilate the spaces open beneath, or by the cargo trunkways which, on our tropical voyage, were left open-sided where they came through passenger accommodation. As far as planning was concerned, there were not only two and sometimes three classes; there was the complexity of special rooms for ladies and for smokers, which we can now eliminate, thanks to changes of social behaviour and improvements in ventilation.

Electric light was a new idea too – my grandfather's method of turning it off

(recorded quite seriously in his diary) was to throw a cloth over it. Electric light made an enormous difference to life on board because of the possibilities of replanning the traditional pattern of the interior once one could easily dispense with natural light.

From the first the accent in passenger ships was on living spaces held in common and on a small personal space, one's own cabin.

To begin with, the cabin was a space which you furnished to your taste. On the *William Metcalfe,* a sailing vessel to Australia in 1839, the passengers were strongly recommended to have their cabin furniture made and fixed before starting the voyage. A Venetian door of jalousies was also strongly advised. This door would, in mid-century, have led straight into the only living and eating space, down the centre line of the ship. Its light was from a central skylight. Along both sides ran the cabins, on the skin of the ship. There can have been very little privacy and precious little comfort here. By 1890, there were public bathrooms for First Class passengers, but water

Dining Saloon of the *Narkunda,* 1920. Skylights and domed ceilings were frequent decorative elements in the first class rooms. Sometimes, even for first class passengers, there was an extra fee for the privilege of entry and this surcharge could exceed the cost of a passenger ticket in steerage.

was not laid on to the cabins, where one still washed in a compactum, a folding contraption of mahogany that shot the used water from its basin into a built-in container down below when you shut it up. We still find its modern counterpart in the *wagons-lits.*

The first break away from the concept of the cabin as a little box, one of a row strung along the ship's side, each with a porthole, came about because ships got so much larger that it became difficult to make good use of the space which had been created behind the row of cabins along the ship's side. The solution was found in an invention of the Bibby Line since known as the Bibby Alleyway. More than half the cabins could now be placed further inboard, to make use of the space there, and yet they could still have private access to a porthole at the end of their private alleyways. Later came the various methods of introducing piped outside air through blowers into inside cabins, and when this was developed further, in the form of conditioned air, cooled and dehumidified, it

was time for yet another development in cabin planning. The only remaining use of the porthole was to see out of. Meanwhile the ships had grown yet larger and more than two rows of cabins could be accommodated along their sides. The Court Cabins were designed to meet these new conditions. All the cabins in a court, thanks to the small upright windows in their own walls, could share the view out through the ship's side.

The cabin is the simplest of the ship's interior design problems, for it poses such specific needs. Greater difficulties come in the large public rooms, where it is much less easy to know what you mean the room to provide for its occupants. It is not enough to provide a series of great rooms with more or less similar features and expect the passengers to make the best of them. Each public room should have a mood built into it and, if the designer is clever, his room will be capable of satisfying more than one sort of mood. The shipowner must lead in deciding what is to be the main purpose of each public room, for it is hard for

123

Anderson, Anderson and Company amalgamated with F. Green and Company to form the Orient Line. The Australian services at the end of the nineteenth century saw the rapid transition from sail to steam. Anderson's recognised the trend and their foresight was responsible for the founding of the Orient Line.

the average designer to know about the daily routine of a large community of seagoing passengers. Of course the designers should be brought into planning discussions at the earliest possible moment, but they should realize that, where the basic design of the vessel is concerned, the Naval Architect must come a very long way before them. Before aesthetics can be considered, his design for the ship must satisfy the stringent safety requirements of the Board of Trade, governing such things as watertight subdivision, stability, freeboard, loadline and fire protection. There are also the rules of Lloyd's Register concerning the strength of the ship and the quality of the materials used in the hull and the machinery. These have an immense influence upon the interior design. This body of regulations is the armature which, by and large, inhibits what might be termed dramatic architectural effects on board. But is drama necessary in the ship interior? Is the sea not dramatic enough? Should not calm elegance and comfort be a more important element in the design of a passenger ship than drama? The answer varies

with the type of voyage for which one is designing. My immediate precursors in the responsibility for the interiors of the Orient Line Fleet had long rejected the usual shipowner solution of that period (I speak of the 1920s), which was to commission a large decorating-cum-furnishing firm to provide sketches for the various rooms in quasi-historical styles. They had found the results of this kind of thing altogether too commonplace to be acceptable. Instead, by 1912, they had commissioned a well-known architect, with a healthy practice ashore, to provide more scholarly architectural interior settings for their ships. This unheard-of innovation had not, as far as I know, been copied elsewhere.

The furnishings were still chosen by themselves, much as they would have furnished one of their own houses. They bought good Oriental rugs for the public rooms, where they were placed on parquet. Chintzes were chosen by them too. Ours being a hot-weather voyage, we still, in the 1920s, had no curtains on board our ships, even in the public rooms. They were said to be stuffy and to collect dirt. The ports or the small windows of the main rooms had wooden jalousie shutters instead, and very bleak the effect was.

These interiors were never accurate period pieces, except I suppose that they were characteristic of 1920. There was scarcely at that date any accepted interior style in this country, except a sort of adaptation of ancient bits and pieces. In the early 1920s a palatial grandiosity still pervaded even the architect-designed rooms I am speaking of. They tended to have classical pillars, rich metal balustrading and a high central area. We were probably the only shipowners who did not provide those favourite shipboard aids to gracious living, armour and baronial stone fireplaces.

On our voyage we had a great range of climates to contend with, and we were better at dealing with extremes of heat than of cold. Draughts are welcome in really hot weather and those rooms were certainly halls of the wind. Hardly any large room was a self-contained unit; it still enjoyed the draughty luxury of an open stairway passing through it,

and these made for winter conditions which we to-day should think intolerable – particularly when, as often, there were doors in these same rooms which opened straight out on to the deck without any intervening lobby. Often to get from one room to another, one had to go across an open deck. It was this that first made me so interested in getting the public rooms more conveniently arranged in relation to each other, which sounds easy enough, but in fact is difficult.

By the early 1930s, my arguments for adopting contemporary interior designs for our new ships became so insistent that my elders evidently decided that there was something in it. But they declared that they didn't feel capable of taking the responsibility for doing so and seeing it through. They declared that I should take over the design responsibility. Even at that date the projected ship was to cost over ten million and we were not in a financial position to make any mistakes over her internal design. My responsibility, they said, was to include the choice of a younger lay architect in sympathy with my intentions. My choice

Above. Detail of an engraved looking-glass (pictured *below*), designed by Lynton Lamb for the first class drawing room of the *Orion*, a ship which represented a radical departure from the traditional.

finally fell upon a man of about my own age, who had as yet done no major work. He remained our chosen architect for the interiors of a series of increasingly large and complex passenger liners for over a quarter of a century. That first ship for which Brian O'Rorke was responsible was the *Orion*. She was delivered in 1935. She has now run her appointed course and has been duly broken up, so she can no longer stand as a witness to the truth of my contention, when the whole project was being argued about before her building ever started, that if she was ahead of the taste of her time when she came into service she would end up her span still well abreast of fashion. But this was exactly what happened.

The interiors of that ship were an unheard of innovation as far as British tonnage was concerned. They represented the reaction from the country-house interior, not so much because an increasing proportion of our passengers were no longer accustomed to country-house life, as because the wheel of fashion had passed on and now dictated quite a different appearance in the rooms of hotels and therefore of ships, which are after all just hotels which take you there as well. The guests in an hotel, however, find the greater part of their entertainment outside it, and often feed outside it as well. It is necessary to provide in a ship a complete environment for living, which means providing rooms that lend themselves conveniently to the various things the passengers may want to do during the twenty-four hours.

What we were seeking to do in designing the *Orion* interiors was not only that, but also to meet the unexpressed need of the travelling public for surroundings that looked more in keeping with the practical achievements of modern engineer constructors. Perhaps subconsciously we sensed the rapidly approaching rivalry of air transport. We were certainly concerned – there is no shame in admitting it – with keeping abreast with fashion, not only fashion in what was considered comfortable living, but in its appearance. Fashion cannot be laughed off as trivial, and there is just as much power, though

it is more subtle, in the visual elements of fashion as in the physical elements of it.

At that date there was no language of interior design, no Design Centre, no shops dealing in standard contemporary fitments (except for a few pioneers concerned with fabrics and light fittings). Often we ourselves had to produce a designer to suggest to a manufacturer the sort of thing we needed, and this concerned a wide range of products at a time when industrial designers were far from being members of an organized professional body, as they now are. Mr. O'Rorke himself designed the furniture.

As far as is known we were the first people to introduce air-conditioning at sea – tentatively at first for certain expensive cabins. It was a real break-through, and has done more than any one other improvement to alter the interior design of passenger vessels making hot-weather voyages. Before its adoption our livelier entertainments had to take place, for comfort's sake, in the open air. There was a large space for the purpose, below decks admittedly, but with open sides which could be shut with long ranges of folding doors in cold weather. In winter these were never as effective as they should have been in quelling draughts, and so the introduction of the internal, air-conditioned ballroom as an addition to the range of normal rooms was a great advance. We had no great desire to change the strange and characteristic shapes of large rooms in ships; shapes dictated by the rhythm of engine-room trunkways, cargo trunkways and other main vertical services. They are a part of being at sea and there is no inherent wrong in that.

SIR COLIN ANDERSON,
a director of The P. & O.
Steam Navigation Company.

R.M.S. ORION
Peter Duff

When, in December 1934, His Royal Highness the Duke of Gloucester pressed a button in Brisbane, Australia, he launched by wireless the Orient liner *Orion,* built for the Australian service at the Barrow-in-Furness, Lancashire, yard of Vickers Armstrongs Limited.

She was a large vessel, with a gross tonnage of 23,371. It was not her size, however, that made her the subject of controversy in many circles. There was something about her appearance that suggested she was a ship of the future. She was not streamlined to any great extent, nor were her lines at all exaggerated; but there was something that set her apart from other liners of her size.

It was unusual for large ocean-going liners to be fitted with only one funnel, and even more unusual to have only one mast. Herein lies the secret of the *Orion's* success. She did not need more than one funnel, so her owners decided that she should have only one funnel.

Main stair of the *Orcades,* designed by Brian O'Rorke. Sister to the *Orion,* the *Orcades* was launched in 1937. Taken over for trooping, her active service proved short and she was lost in 1942.

The Royal Charter awarded to the Peninsular and Oriental Steam Navigation Company.

127

In addition, the absence of a dummy funnel saved the company a further £250 a year for the ship's upkeep.

Such a departure from common practice, such a refusal to accept precedent for convention's sake, showed great confidence and courage. The managers of the Orient Line were looking far ahead, and it is possible that the *Orion* will prove to be the model on which liners of the future will be built.

A similar progressive policy has distinguished the Orient Line from its inception. Its origin was in the firm of James Thomson and Company. In the 'sixties this firm was mainly interested in the trade between Jamaica and Great Britain, which trade consisted largely of sugar, coconuts and rum. In 1863 the style of this firm was changed to Anderson, Thomson and Company, and seven years later it was changed again to Anderson, Anderson and Company.

In 1881 steam vessels superseded the sailing ships which had been engaged in the Jamaica trade. History was made when the new vessels brought bananas into Great Britain in good condition. This was done with the aid of a form of cold-air making machinery, an early type of refrigerating plant. Thus the possibilities of refrigerated cargo were first realized, and now refrigerated meat and fruit ships are an important section of world shipping.

The Australian services at the end of the nineteenth century saw, to a marked degree, the rapid transition from sail to steam. Anderson, Anderson and Company saw the trend of affairs in time and their foresight was responsible for the founding of the Orient Line.

The famous wool clippers of Anderson, Thomson and Company, Devitt and Moore, John Willis, George Thompson Junior and Company, and other firms, were among the undisputed queens of the seas. The first warning of the advent of steam came as early as 1852, when the Peninsular and Orient Company started a service to Australia by the "overland" route. Mails were shipped to Egypt, and thence overland to Suez, for the Suez Canal had not yet been built. A further branch of the P. and O. service ran between Singapore and Australia. This service suffered severe interruptions as a result of the Crimean War, but in 1857 the European and Australian Company started an unsuccessful competitive steamship service.

In 1864, Money Wigram and Sons started a service to Australia with auxiliary steamships which made the single voyage in about seventy days. Unfortunately for them, however, their first auxiliary, the *London,* was wrecked in the Bay of Biscay in 1866. In 1877 Andersons came to an agreement with the Pacific Steam Navigation Company of Liverpool and chartered four of the company's steamships, *Chimborazo, Garonne, Lusitania* and *Cuzco.* Although the Suez Canal had been opened, these vessels for some time continued to use the Cape route. On one occasion the *Lusitania* reached Australia in forty days round the Cape.

These four steamers were acquired in 1878, and the firm amalgamated with F. Green and Company to form the Orient Line. In the following year the Orient Line built its first steamship, the *Orient.* The new vessel, of 5,386 tons gross, was the largest vessel seen in the River Thames since the *Great Eastern* had been launched more than twenty years previously.

With a speed of about 17 knots, the *Orient* was one of the fastest vessels afloat. In 1880 a fortnightly service to Australia was inaugurated and the *Orient* had an active and successful life until she was sold for breaking up in 1909.

In August, 1914, the Orient Line had a fleet of nine ships. Four vessels were lost during the war of 1914-18 and it was not until 1924 that new vessels were built. Since then numbers of fine liners have been built for the Australian service, and their design has necessarily been entirely influenced by the conditions of this trade. As a large part of the voyage, for instance, is made through tropical waters, special precautions must be taken to keep the air in the ship cool and conditioned. In the *Orient* a complete air-conditioning plant has been installed, and she is the first liner to be thus equipped.

The majority of the passengers are British and fond of sports on deck. For this reason there is no indoor gymnasium in the *Orion,*

ornament for ornament's sake, a house, a piece of furniture, a saucepan or a ship becomes purely a machine. It may be a machine for living in, a machine for sitting in, a machine for cooking in, or a machine for travelling across the seas, but in its true form a machine of any kind becomes a thing of beauty in itself. A machine stripped of all superfluous matter is not only a thing of beauty, but is also more efficient as a machine. It was not, therefore, the interests of aesthetics, but the interests of efficiency, that led the owners and builders of the *Orion* to take such trouble over her design.

Everything about a ship should be shipshape. That is not so much a matter of aesthetics as of plain common sense. Yet how many of the great modern liners to-day can claim that their Elizabethan smoking-rooms, their Louis Quinze suites and their modernistic dining saloons are truly "shipshape"? The designers of the *Orion* took a bold step in deciding that from the start she was to be regarded not as a "floating hotel" but as an ocean liner.

For the first time in the history of shipbuilding an architect was called upon to carry out the entire decoration of the ship. At

and the mainmast was suppressed to allow for open-air swimming pools. The boat deck is 278 feet long and 64 feet broad. Here the spirit of the *Orion* is concentrated. More than any other ocean liner of her size, the *Orion* has been planned to be, first and foremost, a ship. It is in this respect that she may claim to be a true representative of the modern movement in art. Stripped of all pretences, innocent of

furniture. The after gallery has sliding windows which can be thrown right open so that the gallery becomes part of the dancing space aft. Farthest aft is the café, which, far from resembling a period drawing-room, is more likely to remind the passenger of an aeroplane.

Outside the café is the verandah, which overlooks the swimming bath on C Deck. The ends of the bath are fitted with special fins which prevent the water from slopping over on to the deck. Two dressing-rooms, with shower baths, are provided for bathers, and adjacent is the tavern, decorated throughout in white, grenadine red and bunting azure.

an early stage the architect, Brian O'Rorke, made many suggestions about the arrangement and planning not only of the public rooms, but also of the cabins, first-class and tourist-class.

The architect's task was a formidable one. The _Orion_ is a large vessel, for she measures 665 feet overall and 630 feet between perpendiculars. She has a moulded breadth of 82 feet and a moulded depth to E Deck of 47 feet 6 inches. Her displacement amounts to 28,400 tons and her draught is 30 feet. Accommodation had to be provided for 486 first-class and 653 tourist-class passengers. Eight decks came under the architect's supervision, and he has made a unique ship of the _Orion_. The main public rooms are situated on B Deck. The lounge is remarkable not for its magnificence and luxury, but for its restraint. The plain ceiling is supported by a number of smooth white columns and is illuminated by concealed lights. The floor, of jarrah and Australian myrtle, is partly covered with hand-tufted rugs by Marion Dorn. The tables are plain and light in colour, and the comfortable chairs are covered in a light blue textile.

Galleries lead from the lounge to the library farther aft. The galleries are not mere passages, for along their outer sides are many alcoves which contain writing desks. Comfortable armchairs and sofas, with occasional tables, allow passengers to sit at ease without disturbing or being disturbed by passing feet. The library is a fine airy room with sycamore

There are fourteen two-berths cabins of the special stateroom type in the *Orion*. They are large rooms, containing two full-size bedsteads and luxurious furniture. There are two cushioned chairs and one armchair of the lounge type, a large dressing-table, and built-in wardrobe furniture. Throughout the ship, bakelite and chromium have been extensively used for decoration, because they are unaffected by sea air.

All the first-class cabins on C Deck are furnished in Australian silky oak. These cabins are fitted with large sash windows which give more air than ordinary port-holes on a run through the tropics where every cubic inch of

moving air is a boon. Similar cabins are situated on D, E and F Decks.

The dining saloons for either class are on F Deck. The first-class saloon is panelled in weathered sycamore, and its central space is lit by concealed lights in a shallow dome. Two of the walls are made up of mirrors. On one of these is sand-blasted a representation of Orion the Giant and his constellation, designed by McKnight Kauffer. Although the ceiling has been lowered by 15 in order feet to house the special ventilation plant, the fine proportions successfully dispel any oppressive feeling. The special air-drying and conditioning plant is unique in the *Orion*.

The tourist dining saloon is similar in many ways, but one wall is made entirely of glass and separates the room from the tourist lounge. Stairs lead up to the café, which is decorated in fawn and blue. A promenade deck encircles this café on E Deck, and right aft are the hospitals in a self-contained deckhouse. An unusual feature of the tourist-class café is the decoration on the central portion of the forward wall. This space is covered by a huge *photomontage,* or collection of superimposed photographs, which forms a striking method of decoration.

Tourist-class accommodation is of almost as high a standard as the first-class accommodation in the *Orion*. Every cabin has

Perspective of the Orient Line *Orontes,* by Brian O'Rorke. Commissioned in 1929, and arch-rival to the P. & O. liners on the same Australian run, accommodation aboard made the *Orontes* a highly popular summer-time cruise ship.

131

cold water laid on, a wardrobe and chest of drawers, a flush panelled door, a specially designed rug, punkah-louvre ventilation and, as in the first class, fire sprinklers. Additional accommodation includes all the necessary spaces for galleys, ironing rooms, laundries and the like, as well as berths for the officers and crew, totalling 466.

Every precaution against fire has been taken throughout the ship. The *Orion* was the first British liner to be fitted with the Grinell sprinkler system, and, in addition, fire-resisting paint has been used extensively.

Water is supplied from a tank in the *Orion's* engine-room. When the level in this tank is reduced, pumps automatically operate and refill the tank from the sea, thus ensuring a ceaseless supply of water for use in the event of an emergency.

On the forecastle deck is the powerful electric windlass with a capstan, driven by electric motors below the deck. Either of these motors is sufficiently powerful to pull up both anchors together. There are two electric warping capstans aft.

The *Orion's* steering gear is of the electric-hydraulic type. Two four-cylinder electric-hydraulic rams are provided; in normal conditions one is kept in reserve. In narrow waters, however, or when docking or carrying out difficult manoeuvres, the second unit can be brought into operation, thus almost doubling the speed of the steering gear. A patent hydraulic steering motor controls the gear from the bridge and there is also a mechanical control on the docking bridge aft.

Two sets of Parsons turbines drive the twin screws of the *Orion* through single reduction gearing. The high-pressure turbines are of the impulse-reaction type, the intermediate-pressure turbines of the reaction type and the low-pressure turbines of the single-flow type. One high-pressure and one low-pressure turbine, working in series, form the astern set.

The speed of the *Orion* is 21 knots. Each of her propellers has four blades of manganese bronze. Each blade weighs 3 tons and has a length of 8 feet from tip to flange, giving a diameter of 19 feet to the propeller.

The six Babcock and Wilcox boilers – four large and two small – are fitted with superheaters and tubular air heaters. All the boilers burn oil fuel under the forced draught, closed airduct system with open stokeholds.

Twelve watertight bulkheads, arranged transversely up to F Deck, divide the *Orion* into thirteen watertight compartments. In the event of the flooding of any of these compartments, it is necessary for the power units and gear, which operate the watertight doors, to be situated well above the highest floodable level.

In the *Orion* the watertight doors are operated on the Scott-Ross system. The power unit is an electric motor. When a door has to be closed, the motor is started and, when it has reached one-third full speed, a patent magnetic clutch automatically comes into operation and connects the motor to the gear which moves the door. This initial force, so created, helps to overcome any form of resistance in the door that may be caused by slight rusting or by a jam in the door itself. From the collision bulkhead to the after end of the propeller shaft, tunnels extends a continuous double bottom. This is divided to form tanks in which fresh water, boiler feed water, ballast and oil fuel are contained. As a further safety precaution, a complete double skin has been arranged between the forward cross bunker and the after end of the engine-room up to the waterline.

Such is the *Orion,* the largest Orient liner. Words and figures can convey only an ordinary impression of the appearance of the ship. She has been designed with the greatest skill.

Meticulous care has been taken to improve the comfort of passengers on the Australian route, not only in such important matters as air-conditioning but also in the smallest detail.

To many people the boat deck is the most attractive of all the decks in a ship. Here everything is shipshape. There are no cocktail bars, no luxurious furniture, no enclosures of glass and mirror. Here is the sea tang, the salt breeze; but not always an uninterrupted view of the sea. In the *Orion,* however, there is an uninterrupted view of the sea. As in many modern ships, the boats are raised on patent davits to well above eye-level so that there is a clean sweep of deck to the rail.

This is only a small point that adds to the comfort, or rather the convenience, of the ocean-goer, but in doing so it adds to the beauty of the boat deck and to the efficiency of the ship.

Although streamlining has not been carried out in the *Orion* to any extent, it is only because it is of no practical assistance. The resistance of the air is immaterial compared to that of the water. Yet the wind can be annoying at times. It may spoil the pleasure of leaning on the bulwarks and looking ahead as the ship glides through the waters. So the forward bulwark on A Deck and on the bridge front is curved and provided with a metal chute. This diverts the stream of air over the heads of those on the deck or on the bridge. This, and similar features, make the *Orion* important, not only because she is one of the largest ships on the Australian run, but also because she is one of the most sensibly designed ships ever built.

MELBOURNE – ATMOSPHERE: A great city with superlatives in the way of racecources and botanical gardens. **TO DO:** primarily race. Secondarily shop, dance, eat, play golf, bathe a few miles away. Motor away to Kosciusko or Murrumbridgee – such trout fishing. **TO EAT:** Mutton, but lobsters as well. And everything you get in Paris. **DON'T MISS:** A thrill at Canberra – the new capital. It's fun seeing the future. **WARNING:** Melbourne is no more Australia than Buenos Aires is Argentina.

Canadian Pacific

ROUND THE WORLD
Harper's Bazaar, 1933

One of the unexpectedly gratifying thrills we obtain from a voyage around the world is that right at the start. Gangways up ! No matter how many transatlantic or interport trips we've been on, this cruise is going to be different. Even the most conservative hearts get that little tingle when they suddenly realise they are off – are actually about to see all those far ports and places. Some of the gallant spirit of Drake, Magellan, and Cook, infuses our veins like wine at the sound of such names as Jaffa Gate, Shepheard's Hotel, Belawan Deli, Bangkok, Bali, Legation Street, Peiping, and the Spanish Main. We suddenly feel that we are actually discoverers – amateurs to be sure, but discoverers none the less. For all those weeks we can comb queer ports and sail new seas, and all the muddle of international affairs can just go hang ! In those four and a half months on board, our lives will swing back four thousand years in footsteps of king and conqueror. It is all a happy dream where

At the end of the 1920's the Canadian Pacific possessed one of the largest Western Ocean passenger fleets. Her *"Empress"* liners sailed from Southampton to Quebec, via Cherbourg, when the St. Lawrence was ice-free, and made long-distance cruises in winter.

133

One of the pioneer passenger motor ships was the Royal Mail liner *Asturias,* built in 1925. Her diesel engines were later replaced by geared turbine propulsion to increase her speed.

everything comes true. We dwell on a floating land of milk and honey: no wrong telephone numbers, obdurate landlords, hay diets, bills, or dust.

As far as world-cruise ships go, the choice is so select that it becomes a matter of itinerary, and how long one can be away. The huge *Empress of Britain* needs no introduction – being the largest vessel launched here since the war and the largest to encircle the globe. She sails from Monaco in January and enters Southampton Water in May – 124 days, and 29,650 nautical miles later. She offers every possible luxury afloat, has an experienced cruise management, a well-planned itinerary and a group of shore excursions which cover the "high spots" east of Suez. That pivotal point which can easily make or mar any cruise, the hostess, is one of the smartest on the seven seas. I have watched her work for the last six years, and to see her handle social events is a revelation in diplomacy, tact, and, energy. There are two orchestras rendering everything from Debussy to the latest "hot" dance tune.

Hamburg-American's good ship *Resolute* is a worthy successor to the historic *Cleveland* of the same line, which made its first world cruise back in 1913. That voyage now is a classic and started a parade of globe-girdling tall ships which has paved its course with more broken engagements and new-born romances; more divorce and potential marriage; more nerves, calm, corkless bottles, and lifelong thrills *per capita* than any other similar period of action on record. Having travelled some 150,000 miles on the S.S. *Resolute* and some 12,000 on her sister ship the *Reliance,* I can briefly outline their chief points.

First and foremost in the tropics one must have a well ventilated, "airy" ship for comfort. The *Resolute* was originally designed for tropical service to South America; her cabin ventilation, broad decks and passageways, and Bibby cabin design give maximum comfort. Her outdoor swimming pool has a glass cover which slides back in fair weather; and sailing eastward into the sun her course strikes each country at just the right season: cool in Cairo and India; just missing the monsoons, cool in

R.M.L. "ASTURIAS"
MOTO NAVE "ASTURIAS"
Thursday, 27th April, 1933.
Jueves, 27 de Abril de 1933.

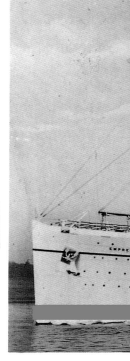

the Philippines, sparkling weather in south and north China, and Japan at the height of the cherry blossom festivals. Japan *can* be miserable in too early spring.

There are two or three other things of note in connection with the cruise. Like the *Empress of Britain* she may be boarded in New York or Villefranche, the latter port on January 28. From this point onward she calls at additional ports, off the beaten track, which bear consideration: Istanbul, or Constantinople; Djibouti in strange French Somaliland – port of the railway straggling over sunbaked and lion-infested desert land to Addis-Ababa, capital of Abyssinia; Belawan Deli and Medan, Sumatra; Chemulpo and Seoul, Korea; Nagasaki and Miyajima – those exotic and most picturesque seaports in southern Japan.

A tariff of £277 is the sum set for the entire cruise round the world, first class, *without* any shore excursions. This naturally includes all accommodation aboard ship and tender service to shore wherever required. All one has to do is advise the cruise management of each port where one has *not* been, and where one would like the advantage of the regular shore

excursions, special trains, advance hotel reservations, and so on, and a nominal additional tariff may be paid. In this way one pays only for what shore activities one actually desires. For those who are making their first world cruise and wish the smooth-running convenience of the *Resolute* shore excursion arrangements, an additional charge of about £110 is required.

And then about seeing odd places like glorious Angkor Wat in Cambodia, and spots like South India. Long experience comes again to aid the traveller. Instead of asking him to embark on the long, dusty railway journey southwards from Calcutta to Madras and South India to meet the ship at Colombo, Ceylon, the *Resolute* does *not* touch at Ceylon first after leaving Bombay. She goes direct to Madras. Here the special, optional, South India party embarks by special train and makes the brief, vastly interesting journey from Madras, via Tanjore, Trichinopoly, Madura, Talaimannar, thence by steamer across the Gulf of Mannar and by motor car to the weird deserted city of Anuradhapura in Ceylon, via Kandy to Colombo, where the steamer has retraced her course from Madras. One glance at a map shows the immense advantage of this seemingly slight change in itinerary.

And now the good old *Franconia* swings into her second Southern Hemisphere cruise – Cunard owned and managed, with face lifted (so to speak) and painted dazzling white from stem to stern instead of the usual Cunard colour scheme. She also offers two tariff plans from Europe to Europe – 405 guineas with shore excursions; 305 without – this last for those who have travelled parts of her route before on other lines and wish to make personal shore arrangements. The total cruise out from New York and back takes about one hundred and thirty-three days, plus ten days or so by fast Cunard transatlantic service. This means that one leaves England late in December with Christmas just over, and returns early in June to be greeted with early English flowers.

Right from the start, this new sort of itinerary veers off from the usual. A touch of British West Indies in Jamaica, and planters' punches at the famous Hotel Myrtlebank! Thence a passage through the Panama, a

chance glimpse of Hollywood's "jungles" of cinema, then the long slant via Hawaii, to Tahiti, Rarotonga, British Samoa, Suva in the Fijis, New Zealand, two Australian ports, then up to Port Moresby through seas positively drenched with romance – of pearlers, blackbirds, pirates and cannibals of not-so-far-gone days. Thence to Kalabahai, and to Bali – which to me is the Garden of the Gods.

One of the main fascinations in world travel is the contrast between homeland and foreign lands. The following list is brief; there are thousands more. No wonder Staff Men are expected to be floating encyclopaedias.

For instance: Panama hats come from Ecuador, Bangkok hats from the Philippines, while balibuntals never saw the island of Bali. In Japan a child is recognised as being a year old when he is born. A waterfall travels uphill near Honolulu. Chop suey was originated in America. Egyptian cigarettes are made from Turkish tobacco grown in Greece, and most Java coffee comes from Africa. The sacred white elephant of Siam is pinkish brown and costs the King thousands a year for food and facials. The Jordan River would be classed as a brook in St. Albans and a Mohammedan policeman with a British automatic pistol guards the Church of the Nativity and the Church of the Holy Sepulchre. In Java a Dutch Wife is not always one to love, honour and obey, but is sometimes a long hard bolster for beds. In Bali, the bridegroom kidnaps his bride the day before the wedding with her father's consent. The Red Sea looks blue and the Yellow Sea grey. An old Cambodian custom permits a husband to kill all his wife's previous fianceés. In India the word "bogey" usually has nothing to do with golf, but is a type of compartment railway carriage.

And then take China. Ladies wear trousers, men wear skirts. Hot drinks not cold are served for cooling effect. Guests at dinner visit first and leave directly after eating. Dessert is eaten at the beginning of a meal. Books are read from back to front; surnames are written first not last. Tea is served with a saucer on top of the cup. White, not black is worn for mourning. Shoes, not hats are removed on entering a house. Flying bats are a symbol of beautiful happiness, and your physician is paid while you are well, never while you are sick.

A Hindu will, if you force him to eat cow, say things about you – but will bless you if it is pork. Mohammedans across the street *vice versa*. The Southern Cross, which has been entwined with romance for longer than a landlord's lease, is neither a good cross nor very expensive. An alibi for young folk to remain on deck after bedtime.

Consider the oddity of everyday names. Imagine being tailored by a chap named Ah Men, or dining in a restaurant run by Hop Fat – both in Peiping. Then consider Mr. Wat He, purveyor of jade; an ivory carver named Hang On who carries on in Hong Kong.

Before we know it our cruise has slipped by. We've paid our Panama Canal toll, and no days, even on sea, can hurry along faster than the last lap after Los Angeles, on the *Empress of Britain* or the *Resolute*. Old Panama and especially Havana, flirt their bright Spanish shawls in our course. Our last tropical cruise port, Havana, is always one of the gayest. The beautiful Casino Nacional is finer than Monte Carlo; the night clubs with their strange *rhumba* music, superfine horse-racing, *daiquiri* cocktails, sea-crab *á la Morro;* a swim at the National pool, or blue sea-water surf at work at *La Playa*. No wonder Havana has been called the "Paris of the West".

Finally, after circling the globe four times, and making shorter voyages here, there and everywhere, I have discovered a few cruise laws which I have listed below.

The Traveller's Code – Do's

Discover the Grand Bretagne Number 2 cocktail at hotel of the same name in Athens.

Go to *Luxor* if the exchequer will stretch. Sunset at Karnak is something not soon to be forgotten, then seek out Aziz Effendi, and command one of his peerless silver fizzes. This also is a ceremony of parts and to be sought after by all men.

Go to Breach Candy for a swim when in *Bombay;* get white suitings made here, and

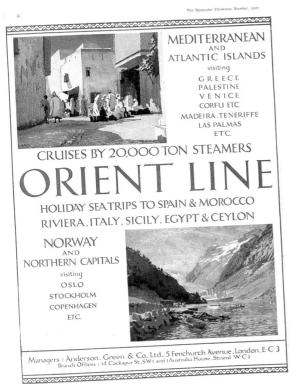
topees for tropics; take an hour and go to the Thieves Market – everything from a harem veil to a Sheffield carving set – and now and again something precious blooming among old sewing machine parts ! Seed pearls, perhaps.

Don't miss frozen coconuts, or handworked silver, when in *Bangkok*. Silver vest and monkey jacket buttons made of coins; very smart. Also dancers' masks.

Swim and dance at Seaview by night, when in *Singapore*. That moonlit drive out from town will conquer even the most congealed heart. Miss not the special gin slings at Raffles, nor malacca canes.

In *Havana* don't miss *Jai-Alai*, the world's fastest game, no matter what else you omit. For the best *daiquiri* cocktail in the world drop into the unbelievably gorgeous salon in the Bacardi Building, and sign the register. Best of all, it is free – with courtesy of the house of Bacardi.

Don'ts

Don't neglect to take enough warm clothing – enough for comfort in England's March – to last you for at least eight weeks of the trip. Mediterranean Holy Land particularly, Hong Kong, Shanghai, Peking, and Japan are all seen during a cool time of year. Be sure to take one heavy overcoat.

Don't buy whites, topees, or monkey jackets before Bombay, where Britain's best tailors locally know what is what and the tariff is sane. Suits made to measure in twenty-four hours ! Nothing worse than a funny Cairo "tourist consumption" topee. Throw 'em overboard after Bali going East.

East of Cairo: Don't eat green salad, drink *any* unpedigreed water, go with head uncovered in the sun, or consume fruits with broken skins. The natives do it, but we can't. The same applies to milk, ices, and butter – anywhere except in European hotels, where the management caters for the British. In and after Japan this ban is lifted on edibles. Wear topees only when, and if, resident Britishers – otherwise an ordinary felt is excellent.

Don't buy any antiques without expert advice; never bargain for any, except unimportant purchases, without someone with you who knows both the merchandise and the local language. He may often get his commissions later from the shops, but it is well worth his slight charge for such services. This applies still more astringently to purchases of gems, jewellery, fine rugs, brocades, and so on.

Don't plan to take all your own scenic photographs yourself. The Cruise Staff photographer will go round and see things you couldn't possibly find the first trip out, and best of all, his price per print in lots of six or eight is far less than your own of equal size.

On tipping – don't go below 10/- per week, per passenger for your table steward and his helper, and for your cabin steward. Any Cruise Staff man will tell you the minimum for the minor functionaries aboard. The ten shilling basis is the lowest minimum possible, and still be fair enough to expect prime service. Of course no steward will say a word even if you pare this down, but remember how hard they work for you.

Don't forget that any world cruise will pack more lifelong memories, genuine thrills, and information into one than any similar space of time or human endeavour. Didn't I get a bride out of it myself, last voyage ? May Allah grant you an equal happiness in one form, or another. *Salaam!*

Destinations various: the shipping lines devised a network of destinations which appealed to the rich and the energetic. In a time when labour was inexpensive, well-to-do travellers felt no constraints as to number, bulk or weight of luggage and a dozen trunks on a journey was not uncommon.

SMARTNESS AND DISCRETION
Frank C. Bowen

To most, a Customs officer is only a man in an unpretentious uniform who seems to take a casual interest in his baggage and have extraordinary luck in dropping on any contraband. There is really little luck about the matter. The Customs officer is chosen for his smartness, and retains his job by maintaining his standard. Above everything, he is a practical psychologist with the knack of putting himself in the place of the traveller who wants to bring ashore a few smuggled goods, not so much to defraud the revenue as to have the excitement and to express the age-old feeling. To this he adds a close observation of the passenger, who can generally be trusted to give himself away.

As a rule, the officer generally sees far more than he betrays. He is allowed to use much discretion, and where the capture does not really matter, except for his own credit, he will occasionally turn a blind eye rather than delay a boat train. At the same time, he hates it to be thought that he has been bluffed, and a bewildered passenger will often find himself dropped on with surprising weight for this very reason.

In addition to his own powers of detection, which are considerable, and the too obvious unconcern of the amateur smuggler, the Custom House officer has the help of many informants who are attracted by the reward paid in the event of detection. Unfortunately, there are no informers about the contraband which is loathed most – dangerous drugs. These are not usually run by amateurs, but by the keenest and cleverest criminals in the game with every device at their disposal. Yet a large proportion of this contraband is stopped at the coast, and most of the remainder is tracked down. The Service is always aiming at stamping out the traffic altogether.

Smuggling by the passengers of cross-channel packets and liners is generally an amateur business, but with the modern tariff it is possible for a certain amount of commercial goods, especially such things as watches, binoculars, lenses, silk clothing and the like, to be slipped in. The smuggling then becomes more serious.

Akin to the officers who examine the passengers' baggage at the port and the railway termini are the hoarding and rummage crews of the waterguard. These two branches join almost every ship coming from overseas. The boarding crew examines the ship's stores, puts any surplus under seal so that it can be used as soon as she leaves British waters, and also does a dozen jobs connected with the legal entry of the ship.

The rummage crew has the more picturesque job – to find goods, which are being deliberately smuggled by the seamen. They have a short time in which to examine with great thoroughness a ship of complicated design, where the crew has been living for some time with every opportunity, if so minded, of evolving the cleverest possible hiding-places for their contraband.

At every dock or wharf which deals with overseas shipping there are officers who examine every pound of cargo which comes out of the ship's holds, and who assess the amount of duty payable. This may not be as picturesque a job as the examination of baggage or the work of the rummage crews, but it has its interesting side. Not only is it difficult to make an exact assessment without delaying the consignment for an unnecessary minute, but also it is an old trick to smuggle heavily dutiable articles concealed in those on which the duty is light.

LUXURY CRUISING
F. E. Dean

High above the Thames, on one of London's tall buildings, there flashes nightly from an electric sign the words "Arandora Star" – conjuring up to the minds of toilers in the great city the vision of a ship that might transport them to the far-off pleasure grounds of the world.

Specially intended for long pleasure voyages to all parts of the globe, the *Arandora Star* is the cruise-ship of the Blue Star Line.

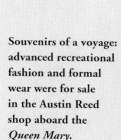

In development of the passenger trade the company decided to inaugurate a cruising service all the year round, and for this purpose the *Arandora Star* was suitably altered.

Cruises are varied in their duration. A voyage to Honolulu may take seventy-five days, but a trip to the fjords of Norway may occupy only a fortnight. Long cruises are available for those with plenty of spare time at their disposal, short cruises to correspond with shorter vacations. Most of these voyages reach seas and territories that link the Empire with Britain's past and the wonderful part played by her seamen in bygone years. The Honolulu cruise of the *Arandora Star* touches on the ports where Drake was wont to call – cities of the Spanish Main. We can, with a little imagination, follow this cruise, starting in mid-winter from Southampton. First we cruise down the English Channel, round Cape Finisterre, and across the Bay of Biscay to our first port of call, Santa Cruz de Tenerife, in the Canary Islands. We have put more than 1,500 miles of sea between our floating home and the great docks of Southampton, and sea and sky have changed – grey to blue, steely chill to the warmth of sub-tropical waters where native divers plunge to the clear depths. Above the port there towers the great peak of Tenerife, 12,100 feet high, which watches over the scene as the great liner's motor launches land happy parties for their twelve-hours stay.

Then off again to the westward. The Island of Trinidad is the next objective and here, off Port of Spain, we stay for most of a day and night before steaming north through the blue waters of the Caribbean to Grenada. Off this lovely island, with its palm trees and its attractive scenery, we pause for eight brief hours and then steam on to Cristobal, gateway to one of man's mightiest achievements – the Panama Canal. To appreciate this triumph of the scientist, the engineer and the humble toiler under their leadership, it will suffice to note the swift passage of the *Arandora Star* from Atlantic to Pacific. A journey of a few hours sees the great liner through the canal.

At Balboa we stay for thirteen hours before the ship steams westward again to the Hawaiian Islands. Enchanted islands these, with golden beaches, palm-fringed, that run down to meet a sapphire sea. Overhead stretches the wonderful blue dome of the sky and everywhere are seen a thousand kinds of tropical flowers – an unforgettable kaleidoscope of colour.

Hilo on Hawaii is visited first – Hilo with its marvellous crescent bay, having the volcanic peak of Mauna Loa, 13,800 feet high, in the background. Here are ancient temples, the famous Boiling Pots, the Kaumana Caves, sugar plantations, the Rainbow Waterfalls, to name only a few of the sights and attractions of this wonderland. Standing by in the bay is our white-walled floating home – ready with every comfort after the strenuous pleasure of sight-seeing is done; ready for the run to Honolulu, on the south coast of Onhu Island.

The very name of Honolulu holds a world of romance. Surf bathing in warm tropical waters, riding in outrigger canoes, viewing tropical fish through the glass bottom of a special boat: these and more are the incidents

Souvenirs of a voyage: advanced recreational fashion and formal wear were for sale in the Austin Reed shop aboard the *Queen Mary*.

A voyage to the antiquities of the Mediterranean in 1857 was said to be the first cruise offered to the public. The *Ceylon,* owned by P. & O., was used for the purpose. By the turn of this century increasing numbers of passengers were finding the time and the resources to make journeys of "recreation and rest" and cruising was no longer the exclusive domain of the "educated and scientific oriented travellers".

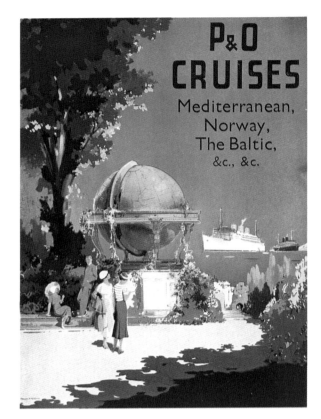

P&O CRUISES
Mediterranean, Norway, The Baltic, &c., &c.

of cruising. More than seventy hours are spent at Honolulu – time in which to visit the wonderful pineapple plantations, and to snatch an hour or two for a trip by aeroplane to the neighbouring island of Maui. Here is the volcano of Haleakala, 10,000 feet high with a crater that measures nineteen miles in circumference, with a drop of 2,000 feet down inside the mountain.

Even Honolulu must be left at last and the steamer sets out for the Golden Gate of San Francisco – where palm trees of tropical islands have given place to the skyscrapers of a vast city. After two days in San Francisco we steam on to Los Angeles and there the ship stays long enough to allow of a visit to Hollywood and Pasadena – passwords, for a few, to fame and fortune in the films.

Then begins the homeward voyage, down the coast of Lower California, skirting the south-western coast of North America to Panama again. Having left the canal behind us we call at La Guaira (Venezuela) and Barbados and then steam steadily eastward to Madeira.

Finally the run home brings us on an April morning to Southampton Water and to a scene vastly different from that we left two and a half months earlier. Winter has given place to spring. Fit and bronzed, we look forward to the wonder of an English summer after a voyage of 22,000 miles. That is but one of the cruises that are accomplished regularly by the

Arandora Star. Sierra Leone and other ports on the west coast of Africa offer yet more variety in the form of native life and tropical scenery.

The Mediterranean, too, offers an endless change of scene – Tunisia, Rhodes, the Dardanelles, Istanbul, Athens, Cyprus, Palestine, Egypt. In contrast with these warm southern beauty spots is the rugged grandeur of Scandinavia, the Baltic and the far North. The Baltic holds a special charm for the cruise traveller.

One specially attractive cruise begins generally at the end of June and lasts for thirteen days. Southampton is left on Saturday and the great port of Hamburg is reached early on Monday morning. Then, after a stay at Hamburg, begins the daytime journey through the famous Kiel Canal from Brunsbattel to Holtenau. Next follows a voyage along the northern coast of Germany to Zoppot, adjoining the much-discussed city of Danzig.

HELSINGFORS – ATMOSPHERE: Sturdy, solid modernity: healthy and unsmiling. **TO DO**: Motor round the most delicious fjord and forest country. Fish. Climb. See castles and the Hall of the Nobles. Sail if in season. **TO EAT**: Drink Schnapps. Eat anything that goes with it. A truffled galantine makes the mouth water, **DON'T MISS**: The engaging friendliness for anything British. **WARNING**: It can be cold. It has, on occasions, been "dry".

From there the run continues to Helsingfors or Tallinn, and thence to Sweden's capital city, Stockholm, where a stay is made from noon on Friday to four o'clock on Saturday afternoon, just one week after the luxury liner has sailed from Southampton. Then begins the homeward run, the next call being at historic Copenhagen, which is reached at noon on Monday. The approach to Denmark's capital is enchanting. When the ship has sailed through the Kattegat the coast of Sweden lies off the starboard beam, and then comes the narrow entrance to Elsinore Sound between shores

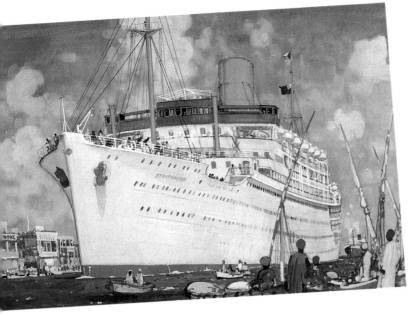

Souvenir Programme

Tropical Follies
1941

ARRANGED AND PRODUCED
BY
THE ENTERTAINMENTS COMMITTEE
BY KIND PERMISSION OF
Col. J. V. R. JACKSON
(COMMANDING TROOPS)

ON BOARD
H.M.T. "STRATHMORE"
AT SEA

COMMENCING
MONDAY, APRIL 28TH, 1941
AT 8 P.M.

PRICE 3D.

Far left. **The decidedly tropical *Strathmore* (completed in 1935), seen here approaching Suez, ran Australian sailings as well as cruises from London and Sydney. The artist, Kenneth Shoesmith, was one of the contributors to the murals on the Cunard *Queen Mary*.**

Left. **The impressment of liners during hostilities was commonplace and saw the *Strathmore* serving as a troopship. Here is a rare programme of entertainment, "Tropical Follies", dating from 1941.**

covered with magnificent beech woods that provide a setting for pretty cottages and fishing villages, and also many fine villas with gardens leading down to the waterside. Sweden is again visited on the run home with a stay of some eight hours at the famous old city of Gothenburg. Tilbury welcomes the travellers home again on Friday morning after a cruise of 2.665 miles.

North of the Arctic Circle

It is from Tilbury that a much longer cruise begins, a voyage of over 5,300 miles which lasts for nearly three weeks. The first call to be made is in the Faeroes. Then follows a brief visit to Reykjavik in Iceland. After she has passed the island of Jan Mayen, the *Arandora Star* arrives at Spitsbergen, or Svalbard, as this northern Archipelago is officially called. Many hours are spent cruising round the bays and harbours of Spitsbergen, and the voyage south begins, past Bear Island to Norway's famous North Cape, the great headland that is Europe's northern outpost. In calm weather the launches of the *Arandora Star* land those who may wish to climb the steep summit with its northern outlook to the desolate Arctic Ocean. Hammerfest is the next port of call, the most northerly town in the world. Surrounded by bleak and barren rocks, the timber-built town is full of interest, and its harbour, thanks to the Gulf Stream, is never closed by ice.

The steamer continues her voyage in this wonderland of mountain, snow-filled gorge and gleaming glacier, still attended by the midnight sun. The beautiful places of call can be described only briefly here. Lyngen Fjord, still north of the Arctic Circle, is within reach of a settlement of Lapps. Next come other marvellous fjords – the great inlets of the sea that twist and turn in the mountains. The greatest of the fjords is the famous Sogne Fjord, 112 miles long, varying in width between two and five miles and believed to be nearly 4,000 feet deep in places.

Into many of these marvellous waterways the *Arandora Star* thrusts her way between the flanking precipices – an unforgettable voyage, amid unspoilt scenes of wild grandeur that has its counterpart only in the entrancing loveliness of the Southern Seas.

HILO – ATMOSPHERE: Colour gone mad. Fairyland and the Witches' cauldron. **TO DO:** Ride. Swim. Go native. Listen to ukuleles sobbing in the shadows. Believe it's real. Spend a dawn at Kilauea. **TO EAT:** Starches, proteins a l'Americaine. Also native dishes – very full-making. Try the local cane spirit, but don't expect to keep your head. **DON'T MISS:** The House of Eternal Fire. Kilauea is an unforgettable wonder. Sit on the edge of the crater and watch the "Goddess Pele's hair" **WARNING**: Don't be cynical. The volcano is worth yawns, dust and the "tourist feeling".

141

THE SHIP BUILDING INDUSTRY
Frank C. Bowen

Before the war of 1914-18 ships were collected in batches in one or other of the anchorages popularly known as "Rotten Row" and periodically offered for sale by public auction. The bidding was supposed to be strictly controlled, certain ships being reserved for national buyers only, whereas others, of smaller importance, could be bought by anybody. The modern routine is quite different. All the sales are conducted by private treaty and any question as to the price realized, whether it is raised in Parliament or outside, is always met with the statement that its divulgence would be against public policy.

After the Armistice there were hundreds of men-of-war to be disposed of, as well as a large number of merchant ships which had been kept in commission beyond their normal life owing to the war boom in freights.

Shipbreakers did well out of the business, but there arose a craze for scrapping and a number of mushroom concerns sprang up all round the British coast.

The price of a ship for scrapping is usually fixed at so much a ton gross for a merchantman and so much a ton displacement for a man-of-war.

The expert eye of the scrapper assesses her value remarkably quickly – bronze propellers, metal in the engine-room, furniture that can be used again and a hundred and one other items.

When there was a glut of steel on the market, and the price was depressed, many shipowners who were hard hit by the slump were obliged to sell their ships for as little as six and seven shillings a ton gross, about the lowest level in the history of the business.

As industry revived, so the price revived as well, the passenger ships being always just a little ahead of the cargo vessels. The £78,000 given for the *Mauretania* worked out at £2 10s. 10d. a ton gross, and the £100,000 which was given for the *Olympic* was £2 3s. a ton.

Shipbreaking is an industry which has grown vastly of recent years and has every chance of further expansion as the demand for steel appears to get bigger and bigger. To the lover of ships there is always something sad about a scrappers' yard where a once beautiful vessel is ruthlessly cut up into lumps of dead material.

SPEED AT SEA
Professor A.M. Low, 1935

It has been suggested that a radical change will eventually take place in the design of passenger-carrying vessels, and that they will be large-scale hydroplanes, travelling at speeds of 60 m.p.h. and upwards. These boats are imagined as streamlined liners, not vastly different in appearance from the latest Atlantic liners, except that they will float on the water and be very much smaller. It has been stated

that a vessel of this type 120 feet long, and with an engine of 4,000 h.p. could do the Atlantic crossing in something over two days, carrying passengers for a fare of £50.

It is all perfectly possible, the one "snag" that I can see being the rough weather. While it might be possible to work a service of these vessels on the South Atlantic, it seems doubtful whether they could stand up to the buffeting of the North Atlantic in winter. Scientifically they are perfectly right – it is ridiculous that ships should waste fuel pushing away water, when they should float on it, and the principle is a very interesting instance of the progress given to other sciences by the discoveries of aviation.

I can well believe that vessels of this type may be developed for special routes and even for warfare, where speed is of prime importance, but it seems doubtful whether shipping as a whole will be radically altered.

On the other hand, it is true that without a huge increase in the size of engines, and thus of the cost of fuelling, it is doubtful whether sea speed can be substantially increased in the near future. It would be dangerous to lay down a maximum speed for any form of transport, but when the effort and money required to bring the average speed for an Atlantic crossing up from the 24 knots to 30 knots is realised, it seems that 40 knots may be a long way ahead. The increased use of light metal alloys in the construction of ships will help, but I cannot see how even this can bring the speed up to that of motor and air transport. The liners must still rely on comfort and economy if they are to stay in business.

ACKNOWLEDGEMENTS

All efforts have been made to contact the copyright holders of any material in this book that
may be in copyright, but Morgan Samuel Editions would be grateful to receive
notice of any copyright material that may have been overlooked.

Morgan Samuel Editions would like to express their gratitude to
the following individuals and organisations who have supplied the
illustrations in this book:

Opposite title page: Tate Gallery; p7, 8/9, 10/11, 15: British Architectural Library/Drawings Collection;
p16: M.S.E./Cobwebs; pp18(top), 19: British Architectural Library/R.I.B.A.; p20: Hulton Picture Library;
p21: P&O London; p23: Hulton Picture Library; p24: M.S.E./Cobwebs; p25: Forbes Magazine Collection;
p27: M.S.E./Cobwebs; p29: Ulster Museum, Belfast; pp30/1: M.S.E/Cobwebs; p32:Sotheby's;
p33: M.S.E./Cobwebs; p35: Caledonia Investments Ltd; pp36, 39, 40/1, 42/3, 45, 47: M.S.E./Cobwebs;
p49: Illustrated London News; pp50/1: M.S.E./Cobwebs; p52: Illustrated London
News; p55: Royal Photographic Society; p56: M.S.E./Cobwebs; p57 (top left): Hulton Picture Library;
p57 (top right and bottom): British Architectural Library/R.I.B.A.; p59: National MaritimeMuseum;
pp60/1 (across top): Hulton Picture Library; pp60/1 (across bottom): Victoria and Albert Museum;
pp61, 62/3: M.S.E./Cobwebs; p64: Columbus Museum of Art, Ohio; pp64/5 (across top): P&O London;
p65 (top and bottom right): M.S.E./Cobwebs; p66: National Portrait Gallery; p72: Sotheby's;
p73: National MaritimeMuseum; pp75, 76/7 (across top): Forbes Magazine Collection;
p77: National Magazine; p78: M.S.E./Cobwebs; pp79, 80/1, 82/3: National Maritime Museum;
pp88/9, 95 (top): M.S.E./Cobwebs; p95 (bottom), 96 (inset): Royal Photographic Society;
pp96 (top), 98/9 (across top): National Portrait Gallery; pp99 (top and bottom right), 100/1, 104:
M.S.E./Cobwebs; p106: Royal Photographic Society; pp108/9: National Magazine;
pp110/1: Illustrated London News; pp112/3: M.S.E./Cobwebs; p114 (top and bottom left):
Illustrated London News; pp114/5 (across top): Hulton Picture Library; pp115 (top right), 118:
M.S.E./Cobwebs; p119: National Magazine; p120: Illustrated London News;
p121: M.S.E./Cobwebs; pp122/3 (across top): Hulton Picture Library; p123 (right): P&O London;
p124, 125 (inset): M.S.E./Cobwebs; p125 (top): British Architectural Library/R.I.B.A.;
p125 (bottom): Hulton Picture Library; p127 (bottom): P&O London;
pp126, 127 (top), 128/9: British Architectural Library/R.I.B.A.; p127 (bottom): P&O London;
p129 (top right): Hulton Picture Library; p130 (top left): P&O London;
pp130/1 (across bottom), 131: British Architectural Library/R.I.B.A.; p132: Royal Photographic Society;
pp133, 134/5, 137: M.S.E./Cobwebs; pp139, 140: P&O London; p141 (left): Ulster Museum;
p141 (right): M.S.E./Cobwebs; p142/3: German Ship Museum, Bremerhaven.

Editor: Robert Saunders
Editorial Assistant: Lucinda Tam
Picture Editor: Mary Roberts
Designer: Tony Paine, Atkinson Duckett Consultants
Publishing Manager: Pip Morgan
Publisher: Nigel Perryman

In addition, Morgan Samuel Editions would like to express
their gratitude for the help of Peter Boyd-Smith Esq., of Cobwebs,
78 Northam Road, Southampton,
without whom this publication would not have been possible